CW00411021

Beatrice's Last Smile

A Journey Through Germany

IQBAL AHMED

To
Victoria Birch,
Best wishes!
Iqbal Ahmed

First Published in Great Britain in 2017 by
COLDSTREAM PUBLISHERS
9 Juliana Close,
London N2 0TJ
coldstream.publishers@hotmail.com

Designed and produced in Great Britain by
Clinton Smith Design

A CIP catalogue record for this book is available from the British Library.

ISBN 978 1 5272 1130 8

This book is dedicated to
Asia, Adam & Arne

Nel mezzo del cammin di nostra vita
mi ritrovai per una selva oscura,
ché la diritta via era smarrita.

Midway upon the journey of our life
I found myself within a forest dark,
For the straightforward pathway had been lost.

Inferno, Canto I
Dante Alighieri, 1265 – 1321

Contents

Port of Hamburg

I was away visiting my aunt's home in Srinagar with my mother when a plain-clothes policeman showed up at our house and informed my father that he wanted to see me to ask a few questions as I had applied for a passport for the first time. It was customary to give a little 'tea money' to a policeman in Kashmir if he took the trouble of visiting someone's home to make enquiries about a passport application. But my father sent him away, telling him he should visit when I was at home. I was only a teenager and perhaps my father didn't consider it necessary for me to be a passport holder. When my aunt heard about my passport application, she found the whole thing very amusing.

People in Srinagar were usually filled with trepidation if a plain-clothes policeman knocked at their door. However, I was eagerly waiting for this one to return. But I wasn't sure if this would be any time soon since he had left our home empty-handed. I was therefore thrilled when he returned the next day. To make himself look more official he produced a small notebook as he sat in our guest-room. After engaging in some small talk, he asked me if I knew a certain man in our neighbourhood who'd been imprisoned for his political views. Yes, I knew the man in question as an acquaintance. My father, who was listening to the conversation close by, put his hand in the side-pocket of his long shirt, took out a couple of notes and placed them in the palm of our guest, explaining that it was for him "to buy a cup of tea". My interrogator's line of enquiry immediately changed and he didn't ask me any more tough questions.

Srinagar was relatively peaceful in that spring of 1987. After a few months, my passport arrived. In fact I was the first person in my family to obtain one. The postman knew there was a passport inside the package he delivered and congratulated me accordingly. I usually gave him a small tip whenever he delivered a letter or parcel but this time I thought he deserved a bigger tip.

The furthest my father had travelled was to Mumbai. It was considered a rite of passage when someone from Kashmir crossed the Pir Panjal mountains in a bus or taxi to travel to Punjab or Bengal for the first time. When I first travelled to Amritsar in Punjab, my grandmother bought me a gift for my maiden voyage.

I didn't quite know when I was going to make use of my passport until, a year later, my cousin asked me if I'd like to accompany him on a business trip to Hamburg. I agreed without giving it a second thought since it at last gave me the opportunity to use my passport. My aunt said it was a good idea after all for me to have applied for it the year before.

I handed over the passport to my cousin to send to his travel agent in Delhi who would have to apply on my behalf for a visa to Germany. I was glad that I didn't have to go to the embassy of the Federal Republic of Germany (as it was then known) to apply for a visa in person. Travel agents in Delhi usually issued dummy tickets (a requirement that proved you definitely intended to travel) until their clients were granted a visa, whereupon you were issued with the real thing.

It was the month of April and I went to a newly opened department store in Srinagar to ask if they sold any warm clothing. The shopkeeper was surprised and asked me why I wanted to buy warm clothes when summer was just round the corner. I explained that I was travelling to Hamburg, which is cooler than Srinagar. Although spring in Srinagar is very pleasant Kashmiri people like to wear layers of clothing because it takes them a while to shake off the winter chill. The shopkeeper told me it was my lucky day because he had some warm clothes in stock.

I hadn't been inside an aircraft until I took my first ever flight from New Delhi to Frankfurt, the connecting link in our journey. I had only travelled by road from Srinagar to Amritsar and the capital city of Delhi. It was a McDonnell Douglas aircraft operated by Lufthansa. The stylised blue crane on the yellow tail of the plane suggested a smooth swift flight. As a child, I had heard someone say that an Airbus was going to arrive in Srinagar one day, which made me wonder what a big bus had to do with air travel. The word 'airport' must have sounded similarly odd at first, perhaps causing people to wonder about the connection between 'air' and 'port'. I heard older people in Srinagar calling our civilian airport an *aerodrome* since it was and still is operated by the military. But they pronounced the word as 'aide-room' because it was easier that way.

The heat in Delhi in May was oppressive and my cousin and I spent just a few days in the town preparing for our trip to Hamburg. A businessman from Kashmir who lived in Delhi told me that whenever he travelled there in the spring the first thing he did on arrival at Srinagar Airport was unbutton his shirt in order to be embraced by the refreshingly cool air.

I had to collect my passport and air-ticket from my cousin's travel agent who was from Kashmir and had worked for a travel agent in Srinagar before opening his own ticket agency in Delhi. When I went to collect my ticket, I found him among other agency staff, sitting in a glass cabin at the far end of his office. It was midday and hot food arrived from his home in a stainless steel tiffin box. My cousin thought the agent has done well because he was only in his twenties. His father was a retired civil servant who came to the office for a few hours every day to help his son with bookkeeping. There were a couple of clients in his office when I arrived, haggling with him over the price of an air-ticket. It was quite usual for customers to haggle over the price with New Delhi travel agents in those days.

We travelled to the international airport in Delhi late at night and paid a fee to fly to Frankfurt where we were to pick up our connecting flight to Hamburg. But the Delhi-Frankfurt flight was delayed, which meant that we missed our flight to Hamburg. There was a businessman from Srinagar on board who was delighted the flight was delayed because it meant getting a free room for a night at a four-star hotel at Frankfurt's airport. He said that he had travelled to Frankfurt a year ago on a delayed flight and had been given a room at an airport hotel where they served smoked salmon for breakfast. I'd never eaten salmon before and had no idea that fish could be served for breakfast as well as for lunch and supper. Our fellow-Kashmiri informant told us that we didn't even need to leave the airport at Frankfurt but could walk straight into the hotel from the arrivals hall at the terminal. And so it turned out to be.

When we arrived in Hamburg we stayed at the home of Sharif, a businessman from Afghanistan who visited Srinagar often and was one of my cousin's clients. I'd become acquainted with him there, in fact. He had a house in Hamburg and another in the country, which he used at weekends. In younger days he had done a business administration course in a German university and was one of the very few Afghan businessmen to settle in Hamburg in the 1960s.

I would have liked to explore Hamburg but I was accompanying my cousin and therefore went with him wherever his business took him and got to see a bit of the town that way.

Sharif usually stayed in a hotel on the Boulevard of Lake Dal in Srinagar. One day when he was visiting the town a bomb went off in a public urinal outside his hotel. I met Sharif that evening but he seemed oblivious of the day's dramatic event. When I mentioned the incident to him he said that it wasn't a bomb – more like a firework going off. I had seen the damage caused by the bomb and it had destroyed the urinal beyond repair. He said that if a small blast like that happens in Kabul the grazing goats near the site don't even lift their heads and just keep on grazing.

Sharif drove us to his home in a Japanese car. I would have expected it to be German-made but he said it was more economical to drive a Japanese vehicle. The beige-coloured seats in his car smelt of new leather and it looked plush compared to the Ambassador car owned by my father which had seats made of faux leather. Sharif lived in Blankenese in Hamburg, an affluent neighbourhood on the banks of the river Elbe. His house had three floors – two and a half above ground and one half under. The lower ground floor of the house was used to accommodate guests. He said it was obligatory in Kabul to host your friends and relatives at your home if they were visiting town. Sharif had an old friend who'd been living at his home in Hamburg for years. He was older than Sharif and wore such a long white beard that many kids in the neighbourhood called him 'Opa', which means 'grandfather'.

Everything looked very orderly and pre-planned in

Germany compared to the few days I spent in chaotic Delhi. The buses and cars in Hamburg glided along the roads making very little noise, unlike those in Delhi and Srinagar, which made a horrendous racket. I had taken a ride in a Phatphati from New Delhi to the old city and its deafening noise kept buzzing in my head. I marvelled at the ingenuity of the person who had originally put together a diesel-engine motorbike with a rickshaw. It belched black smoke.

In the evening, Sharif took us to his local swimming pool, which he frequented twice a week. It was a long, crowded pool and Sharif jumped into one of the lanes and swam like an otter. This was the first time I'd ever set foot inside an indoor swimming pool, having only swum in the open air in Lake Dal. It was overwhelming to see so many swimmers in such an enclosed space. I had once accompanied a relative to a hotel in the centre of Srinagar that had a swimming pool in its back garden. The swimming pool was hidden from the sight of people entering the hotel lobby by a wooden fence. Peeking through a gap in the fence, I could see the reflection of a woman in a swimming costume in the azure water of the pool. That image stayed fresh in my memory for many months. There were many couples in the pool in Hamburg and some of them were kissing and hugging in the water.

I had once hired a small Gondola-like boat known as a Shikara to cross Lake Dal and rowed it to the middle of the lake with a friend in order to swim from a pavilion-style barge (called 'Shamrock', as I recall – another was called 'Rolls

Royce') which was used by foreign tourists holidaying on the houseboats in Lake Dal. The barge owners did not usually allow the local men to rub shoulders with their foreign guests. The top-deck of the pavilion was used for sunbathing by European and American tourists hidden from the sight of the boatmen who rowed them across in their Shikaras. However, to our surprise we were allowed to use the swimming facilities on one of those barges. After we'd swum, I went up with my friend to the top deck of the Shamrock barge and saw a woman in skimpy swimwear lying flat on the wooden floor of the top deck, caressed by the sun. My friend whispered that the Memsahib was German. How did he know? He pointed to a pair of Birkenstock sandals by her side. But I was doubtful that someone could tell the nationality of a foreign woman simply by the sandals she wore until the Shamrock's owner divulged that she was indeed German.

Sharif was in his 60s and didn't have any children. Instead, he took care of his sister's family whose husband was killed in Kabul a few years after Soviet troops invaded Afghanistan. She and her children had lived in Peshawar in Pakistan for a few months before Sharif brought them over to Hamburg. Sharif's nephews and nieces were all grown up and attended various vocational colleges in Hamburg. His oldest nephew, Faizullah, called Faiz for short, was doing a mechanical engineering course and the younger one attended an electrical engineering college. His nieces were doing a catering course.

The men in the house gathered in the evening in a living room on the ground floor whereas the women stayed on the upper floor if there was a male guest in the house. My cousin and I joined Sharif and his elderly live-in friend, Opa, for a game of cards. Faiz advised me that Sharif didn't like to lose and I should keep my cards close to my chest. Faiz had visited Srinagar with his uncle, which is where I'd met him for the first time. As a matter of fact, one of Faiz's ancestors had ruled over a vast swathe of the Indian subcontinent from his base in Kandahar a couple of centuries ago.

Faiz usually helped his uncle in the warehouse in the afternoon after finishing his college work. I asked him which company he was going to work for after finishing college. "Mercedes", he said, "if they give me an opportunity to work for them".

At the weekend Sharif drove us to his second home, which was in the countryside. Along the road we saw white cottages with thatched roofs. Each cottage had an orchard at the rear as part of its estate. Whereas Sharif's house in Hamburg was built around the time he arrived in the city, in the 1960s, his home in the country turned out to be one of these old cottages.

I wanted to get some fresh air and decided to take a walk. As I passed a few white cottages, I saw a man running very fast towards me, pursued by a police car. The man jumped over a wooden fence and disappeared behind the trees in an orchard. The policemen got out of their car, realised they had lost him and gave up the chase. He looked like a Moroccan and since someone in Hamburg once asked me if I was from Morocco. I was worried that the police might suspect me of being an accomplice of the fugitive. Luckily I carried my passport with me and was ready to show it to the policemen. But they took no notice of me, got back into their car and drove off. When I told Sharif about it he said that there was no need to carry a passport with me while I was in Germany.

We spent the weekend at Sharif's country cottage. He liked to tend his orchard and cook food at the weekends. He was an expert when it came to cooking Afghan food as he'd been briefly married to an Afghan woman when he was in his thirties. Someone in Kashmir once told me that Sharif had divorced his wife because she put too many onions in her dishes – unusual grounds for divorce. Whenever he visited Kashmir, Sharif liked to buy Madeira cakes at a bakery near Lake Dal in Srinagar and take them with him to put on his breakfast table in Hamburg.

There were also many varieties of German bread on the breakfast table. Faiz urged me to try the brown bread with quark. I was unaccustomed to such a rich variety of food at breakfast time and knew I couldn't keep up with my host's family. But Faiz disliked the idea of wasting food and considered it sinful to throw leftovers into the garbage bin. "Eat whatever's on your plate and don't worry too much about putting on weight. There's a basketball court on our front lawn."

On Monday morning Sharif drove us to his office in Freihafen near the port of Hamburg. We drove over a bridge on a waterway and then along a cobbled road to reach his office, which was on the upper floor of an old warehouse. There was a rich aroma of coffee in the air since some of the warehouses stocked sacks of coffee beans. The lower floors of Sharif's office building were occupied by other Afghan businessmen. Though the building was over a hundred years old, Sharif's own premises were equipped like a modern office. There were two men working there. One of them was from Kandahar and the other from Herat in Afghanistan. Yet another employee in the warehouse was from Kabul. The warehouse was accessible from the side-wall of the office through a sturdy iron double door. It was a huge hall, full of merchandise imported by Sharif from various Asian countries. Faiz showed me around the warehouse and opened a window at the back for me to see the waterway from which the goods were once loaded, using chains and pulleys, when the warehouses were built more than a century ago. We suddenly heard an announcement on a loudspeaker and when we looked out of the window I saw a boat full of tourists being guided through the waterways. They were looking up in wonder at the old warehouses and some of them waved when they spotted us perched at the window.

I asked Faiz how they brought up the heavy pallets of goods since the pulleys were no longer in use. He told me to follow him and showed me a loading bay at the front of the building fitted with electric lifts. The sea-containers were loaded onto trucks at the nearby port before these trucks docked at the warehouses and their cargo came up in the lifts that moved up and down in open shafts. I could see the sacks of dried fruit being loaded onto the floor below Sharif's office. Faiz told me that the owner of the business below had a few more warehouses in the Freihafen. I had seen him entering his office, looking rather like someone from Uzbekistan. Sharif had greeted him and told me that he came from a town in Northern Afghanistan that was indeed close to Uzbekistan.

Sharif had been running his business in Hamburg for almost 30 years. He had worked for Bank-e-Millie Afghan (BMA) in Kabul before becoming a businessman. Sharif's assistant from Herat proudly claimed that BMA was founded by a businessman from his home-town. Sharif had done a business course in Hamburg before setting up an office in the Freihafen. Since Hamburg is a port city and Afghanistan is landlocked he found it quite bizarre to see a sea-container bearing the name of a German shipper, 'Schenker', on a truck driving through Afghanistan. I had heard of this shipper many times in Srinagar and had wrongly believed that it belonged to an Indian business named Shankar.

A waiter from a local Afghan restaurant arrived at noon with food for everyone in Sharif's office. Faiz explained that this neighbouring restaurant sent them food every day but did not charge anything for it since the building that housed the restaurant was owned by Sharif and he had given a part of the ground floor to an Afghan family to open a restaurant in it in order to help support them. Sharif also supported a few other Afghan families who had arrived in Germany after the Soviet occupation of his country.

The Afghans who lived in Hamburg in the 1970s were mostly well-to-do businessmen. But the people who were forced to leave Afghanistan after war broke out between the Soviets and Afghan fighters during the 1980s were very different. They had gone to live in refugee camps in Pakistan and Iran, and were down and out, except for those who were lucky enough to have a relative in Europe or America and managed to travel there. Many Afghans had arrived in New Delhi by air and then travelled to live in Mumbai or Bangalore.

Faiz had lived with his family in Peshawar for six months after his father was killed and found it a humiliating existence. His uncle had moved heaven and earth to bring them over to Hamburg. Sharif knew the chances of peace in Afghanistan after the arrival of the Soviet tanks were slim and didn't want his sister's family living in a camp in Peshawar forever.

Faiz had felt insulted when he was quizzed by a thin moustachioed immigration officer at the International Airport in Lahore. He was catching a return flight from Lahore and didn't realise that his German travel document had expired the day before. He was lucky to be accompanied by his uncle, who was a German passport holder and made a big fuss at the counter until the officer let them board a flight.

I met Sharif's other nephew at his office. He was a quiet young man who didn't talk much. When he broke his silence after half an hour it was to remark in Urdu that the weather in Hamburg was very bad. Faiz had told me earlier that his cousin was suffering from depression because of the weather in Germany, which surprised me as I hadn't known at the time that there's a correlation between depression and bad weather. One of Faiz's acquaintances sitting in the office came from Mazar-e-Sharif in Afghanistan. He said that he walked down streets of sorrow in Hamburg and his home-town was a paradise. I had seen pictures of the dusty roads of Mazar-e-Sharif, which some people believe is the burial place of Imam Ali, the son-in-law of Prophet Muhammad, and regarded as the first spiritual leader of Shia Islam. The place did not look appealing but for a displaced person it was a veritable paradise. The word Mazar means 'mausoleum'.

Sharif's office had become a meeting place for Afghan exiles in Hamburg. The man from Herat who worked in Sharif's office wore a black shirt and black trousers and was very well-groomed. An Afghan man visiting Sharif asked the man jokingly why he was dressed all in black like a Shia Muslim – the colour that Shia clergymen usually wear to commemorate the massacre at Karbala 14 centuries ago. The Herati man replied that he was indeed a Shia Muslim and the visitor swiftly changed the subject.

The man who worked in Sharif's warehouse had a greying brown beard and kept a copy of the Koran in his pocket. He sat by the window at the back of the warehouse reading the holy book when he wasn't busy packing and unpacking the merchandise. Another Afghan, in his early twenties, was running errands for Sharif and other businessmen in Freihafen. He told me that he was living in a *Sozialwohnung* – a council flat – and had no relatives in Hamburg.

Faiz had fond memories of his childhood in Kabul. His father had been well-respected since he worked as an engineer for a government department and people in the town always addressed him by his professional title. Faiz's family led a privileged life in Kabul until his father was killed by a stray bullet in a battle between Soviet troops and Pashtun fighters. The family fled from Kabul to Peshawar and lived a destitute life in a camp there. "I can never forget that experience," Faiz said. "It changed my outlook on life forever. It made me aware how our fortunes can change in a moment and turn well-respected people in one's own country into pariahs in another. Many people in Europe and America like Afghan hounds more than they like Afghans displaced by war."

When Sharif saw his nephews and nieces in a Peshawar refugee camp, he was distressed by their wretched appearance. They had travelled by a pick-up van from Kabul and then on foot to reach Peshawar, surviving on dried peaches on this treacherous journey. After six months without a haircut Sharif's nephews looked so bedraggled that he took them to a barbershop straight away and then bought shoes and clothes for his sister's entire family.

Faiz showed me a picture of their family house in Kabul.

It was a three-storied building surrounded by a considerable amount of land. Someone who had recently travelled from Kabul told him that his ancestral home had been hit by a shell and reduced to rubble. The UN had provided tents for the camps but even basic facilities like drinking water and toilets were scarce. It was tough to live in a tented camp for six months. On top of their material hardships, the refugees feared bombardment by Soviet warplanes during the night.

Faiz and his siblings sometimes ate only one meal a day in Peshawar and when they arrived in Hamburg they were shocked to see how much food went into rubbish bins every day. They didn't like the idea of wasting food so there were usually no leftovers on their plates at mealtimes. Faiz said that he found it bewildering in the beginning to see the ripe and ready fruit that had fallen to the ground in the orchards around his uncle's country home. He collected all the fallen apples in Sharif's orchard and his mother made apple jam and distributed it in bottles among the Afghan families living in Hamburg. Faiz's mother also cooked pilau rice with raisins once a week and sent it to a mosque in Hamburg where many Afghan men went for Friday prayers.

Faiz felt great sympathy for some of the Afghan men living in Hamburg who had arrived in Germany without their families because his only consolation while living in the camp in Peshawar was that at least he was there with his family. But it was like living in a no-man's-land and he considered himself lucky that he had an uncle who had already settled in Germany. Some of the Afghan families living in Peshawar suffered the misfortune of separation, each member travelling to a different country. It remained a distant dream for those families to be together again.

To forget their sorrows, some of the Afghan men living on their own in Hamburg smoked opium. The opium poppies are grown in Afghanistan and I was puzzled how these men obtained opium in Hamburg. Faiz asked one of the Afghan men who came to their office if he had some opium on him. The visitor took a small sachet out of the inside pocket of his jacket and as a goodwill gesture urged Faiz to take it. Faiz didn't even smoke cigarettes. But he knew opium was a painkiller and a German friend had told him that it used to be sold by apothecaries in Hamburg. I could see the sadness in the eyes of the man who carried opium in his pocket and I realized that he wasn't using it for recreational purposes but to forget the pain of a lost homeland.

Although Faiz had arrived in Hamburg only a few years ago he had made many friends, thanks to his uncle's philanthropic work. He also went to college. But some of the Afghan men who came to his uncle's office were without work and didn't know how to spend their days in Hamburg. I asked the man who was running errands for Sharif what other haunts he frequented in the city and he told me that he often went to a Burger King restaurant to fill his day and hoped that one day he would have a girlfriend and would take her there for a meal. He was twenty-six years old and saw a lot of teenage boys and girls eating in the fast food restaurant after school hours. He spoke very little German and couldn't strike up a conversation with anyone in the town.

The college Faiz attended was having a gala day and he asked me if I wanted to come along. He was going to wear a tuxedo but told me it was okay for me to wear casual clothes. There was to be a concert and a lot of activities taking place in the college grounds. I heard the audience shouting "zugabe, zugabe!" which meant, so Faiz told me, that they wanted the band to play more music. As we walked through the college grounds, one of the sports teams was celebrating a win by shaking a huge bottle of champagne. Faiz accidentally got drenched in it and felt irked that his new tuxedo was soiled.

Fortunately, he had escaped far worse discomforts.

St Pauli Pier on the Elbe

I would have liked to stay in Germany for a few more days to explore Hamburg but my cousin didn't yield to my request since I was meant to be accompanying him on his business trip. 'What would I tell your mother,' he said, 'if I left you behind and something happened to you?' I hadn't really thought about it but since my cousin was older than me he considered it his duty to bring me back safely with him. So we toured a few more countries in Europe for two and a half weeks.

On my return to Srinagar, I heard that some people had protested about the constant blackouts due to power cuts and one of the protestors had been shot dead by the police. The protests about the lack of electricity were a constant occurrence during my childhood, but as children we didn't mind so much the power cuts on weekdays as we did those that occurred at weekends. It was upsetting for children and adults alike if there was an unscheduled power cut on a Sunday evening when the only TV station in Kashmir would broadcast a Bollywood film.

During the winter months there was no electricity half the time because the hydroelectric power stations in Kashmir produced less electricity when the snow-fed rivers dried up. Therefore our electricity provider turned off the power of each neighbourhood in Srinagar on fixed days of the week in order to reduce the load. But a blackout on a Sunday was usually rotated so that people living in certain neighbourhoods weren't deprived of watching a much-loved Bollywood film if their fixed day for the power cut happened to be a Sunday.

Children in one neighbourhood would often go to a relative's house in another neighbourhood to escape the power cut on a Sunday night. But watching an entire film on television for three and a half hours was also a matter of luck because it depended on a continuous supply of electricity. There were power failures for short periods during the course of an evening due to faulty transmission lines. The children in my neighbourhood would gather outside a small substation to see if a lineman could fix it and then run back to their homes if he succeeded in repairing the fault. If he didn't have any luck, the disappointed children would picket outside the station until late at night. I once heard an Englishman at a hotel in London describing to a fellow guest a power failure that lasted a few minutes as "a massive cut" – quite an exaggeration compared to the power cuts in Srinagar that sometimes lasted for days on end.

During the two years that followed the return from my maiden visit to Hamburg, the Valley descended into turmoil and in early 1990 a continuous curfew was imposed in Srinagar for many weeks. It was during this troubled period that my uncle asked me if I wanted to travel to Hamburg again, this time to act as his business representative since he still had a few clients in Germany. My cousin thought that this invitation to live for a while in Germany was most fortuitous. As for me, since I was going to travel to Hamburg on my own this second time around, I thought that at the very least it would give me a chance to explore the town more fully.

It was early spring but there was no joy left in Kashmir to welcome the new season and I travelled to Delhi in pensive mood. From my coach I saw villagers along the way rounded up by the security forces and obliged to sit by the roadside until the soldiers finished searching their homes. It was a sad spectacle and I felt guilty to be travelling in a bus through villages that had been cordoned off, their inhabitants gazing at passing vehicles in despair.

I decided to take a camera with me to Germany and was advised to register it with a customs officer at the international airport in Delhi so that I could bring it back without incurring duty. I had to ask for an officer to write the make and type of the camera on my passport and was able to find such a qualified personage only with difficulty. He came across as very authoritative, looking me up and down before entering the camera details on one of the last pages of my passport.

Smoking was still allowed during flights but smokers were relegated to the back rows so you could see swirls of smoke rising to the ceiling at the back of the aircraft. Many passengers on long-haul flights clapped when their aircraft touched down on the runway. It was a common courtesy in those days to engage in conversation with fellow passengers. I had a long chat with a person sitting next to me, a retired civil servant who told me that he loved to travel and was on his way to California via Frankfurt to see his daughter.

I stayed at Sharif's home for a few days while looking for a room to rent in Hamburg. He was away on a business trip so it was Faiz who hosted me at his uncle's home. I wanted to find a room as soon as possible so that I didn't overstay my welcome there. I found a room advertised in a letting agency and made an appointment to see it. It was to my liking – it had a large window and a high ceiling – and I paid a month's rent in advance.

After moving to this accommodation, I soon realised that I had rented a room in the infamous Reeperbahn neighbourhood of Hamburg. I felt too embarrassed to let Faiz and others know this and told them it was Königstrasse, which is one stop from Reeperbahn on the train line. I had to walk through a street flanked by clubs advertising live sex shows to get to the train station. The name of the street was Grosse Freiheit, which means 'Great Freedom' – a name that baffled me. One of the nightclubs there displayed pictures of the Beatles at its entrance since they had performed at the venue during their time in Hamburg. I had heard their name from one or two of their ardent fans in Kashmir but had no idea what the band members looked like until I saw their pictures on a wall in Hamburg.

I kept up my pretence if anyone asked me where I lived in the city. There was a solitary church among the sinful places in this neighbourhood. I learnt later that Reeperbahn was nicknamed 'the most sinful mile'. On my daily walk to and from the train station, I passed a middle-aged woman who always stood near an ice-cream vendor. He wore a thick moustache and a white coat like a doctor and the woman who stood near him wore bright pink lipstick and carried a shoulder bag in a matching colour. It took me many days to realise why she loitered there. Most of the time she stood there silently but sometimes I saw her chatting to the ice-cream vendor. On some days I saw her standing at the same spot when I returned home after many hours away, having seen her earlier on my way to the station. There was also a towering man who stood outside a club door. He wore a suit and a bow tie, attire that seemed to me to be at odds with his line of work. Sometimes I felt disposed to nod my head in acknowledgment of such familiar faces in Grosse Freiheit.

The house I lived in had a big wooden door that opened onto a stairwell. I shared the flat with a Japanese man and a German woman. The Japanese man smoked something very strong that knocked him out and sometimes he would fall asleep sitting on the toilet seat. The German woman called me by my last name and one day knocked at the door of my room to tell me that she had washed a rubber mat lying at the entrance to the flat and wanted me to contribute towards its cost. I assumed this would be a hefty amount but she said that I owed her one and a half marks, which was less than a pound. I was surprised that she bothered to ask her flatmates for such a paltry sum.

Grosse Freiheit looked desolate in the early morning after its bright neon signs faded into daylight. But I saw a few tourists with cameras slung around their necks walking leisurely up and down the street. One day I drifted into a screened-off side-street where I used to see men trickling out from behind the screen. I saw a succession of women in lingerie sitting on leather chairs within their glass-fronted domains. Their white lingerie became fluorescent under the ultraviolet light. It was a shock for me, like seeing Eugene Delacroix's painting, *The Death of Sardanapalus*, for the first time. The men in the painting are fully clothed whereas the women are lying nude.

My daily commute took me to the Hauptbahnhof, the main train station, and from there I took a walk to Sharif's office in Freihafen. I would usually pass a long row of men, with a few women among them, sitting outside the station drinking cans of beer to while away the time and looking at passers-by in drunken stupor. I also passed a man and a woman standing outside the station handing out copies of a Jehovah's Witness magazine. They greeted me politely in German every time I passed them. It was a bizarre journey from my rented room behind the Reeperbahn to Sharif's office, passing such people as the woman who wore bright pink lipstick and the respectable-looking JW couple.

I spent my working hours in Freihafen. Wanting to buy

a small radio to listen to the news from home in the evenings, I followed Sharif's suggestion that I go to an electronics store called Brinkmann, a huge store that sold everything from small radios to satellite dishes. I was thrilled to see a portable satellite dish that could be fitted to the exterior wall of a house. I had only seen two giant satellite dishes in Kashmir – one at the bottom of a hill in Srinagar and the other on top of a hill outside the city – and I wasn't sure if those dishes were used for scientific or military purposes.

The small radio kept me informed about goings-on in Kashmir. I also went to a library in Hamburg where I'd found a copy of an English language newspaper, *The Guardian*, in its reading room that published the occasional news report on Kashmir. I noticed the name of the British broadcaster, Zainab Badawi in the TV listings. Many years later, I bumped into her in Hampstead. She was crossing Heath Street and I was cycling down the hill. She stopped and apologised to me. But it was I who should have stopped and apologised.

Faiz showed me the shop in Jungfernstieg where he had bought his tuxedo for the gala day at his college. It is one of the main shopping streets in Hamburg, along Lake Alster, which is divided into two parts – Inner and Outer Alster – like Lake Dal in Kashmir, also divided into a larger and a smaller part. But Alster is an artificial lake whereas Dal is a natural one.

I saw a department store that had the name 'KAUFHOF' displayed above its entrance and recalled a businessman in Kashmir who was renowned for having sold merchandise to this store 20 years ago. Faiz said that his uncle likewise purchased clothes for everyone in their family from a wholesaler at discounted prices.

I walked past an ornate building a few times that made me wonder what was housed in it until Faiz told me that it was called 'Rathaus' – Hamburg's town hall. I also noticed such banks as Commerzbank and Deutsche Bank, names I was familiar with because my cousin mentioned them whenever he went to see his business banker in Srinagar. He once told the banker that, unlike people from Kashmir, his German clients could withdraw money from any branch of their bank and didn't have to go to the particular branch where the account was based.

I popped into a branch of a German bank with Faiz when his uncle sent him there to withdraw some cash from a business account. The cashier handed him a neat wad of notes that looked as if they'd been printed on the premises. Banks in Kashmir usually give new notes to their account holders only twice a year, on the occasion of Eid, a bi-yearly Muslim holiday when adults give cash to children as 'Eid money'.

Travelling home in the evenings was a dislocating experience, like being transported from a neat and tidy model town to one consisting entirely of grunge. After living in this notoriously grubby district for two months, I was lucky enough to find accommodation in another neighbourhood on the outskirts of Hamburg. It happened that an Afghan acquaintance of Sharif called Zahir, who was a doctor by training, came to see him at his office and mentioned to him that he was looking to rent one of the two rooms in his flat. I realized it was my only chance to move out of the Reeperbahn area. What's more, Zahir said that I could pay the rent at the end of the month and didn't need to pay a deposit.

Zahir was working in Hamburg but not as a doctor. He was a bookkeeper for an Iranian businessman in Freihafen. Now in his late thirties, he had worked in Kabul for ten years as a qualified doctor before arriving in Hamburg with his wife and two children. Travelling through several countries, they had finally boarded a flight from Bangkok to Frankfurt, a journey he described as hellish. They had arrived at Frankfurt airport without visas. He had spent all the money he possessed on their perilous journey from Kabul via Thailand to Frankfurt. Only two years later he and his wife became estranged and the couple separated.

I asked Zahir the reason for the separation. "I've been searching my soul since then," he said, "to figure out what went wrong between us. She cut her hair short and wore velvety boots after we separated." He thought perhaps it was the hardships he had faced by not being able to work as a doctor that resulted in the breakup of his relationship. He had done odd jobs in Hamburg and couldn't find the time to pass the necessary exams to work as a doctor in Germany. It was challenging enough for him to learn a new language from scratch, let alone pass a medical exam in it.

In the beginning, Zahir had worked in a fast food

restaurant. He mopped the floor and cleaned the toilets. He couldn't work behind the counter there because he was unable to communicate with customers in German. He had dreamt of a better life in Hamburg but it had turned out to be a nightmare. Zahir had the same name as the deposed king of Afghanistan, Zahir Shah, who lived in exile in Rome, and like his namesake he felt melancholy about his reduced circumstances. I heard him listening to the songs of an Afghan singer, Ahmad Zahir, who had died in 1979 – the year in which Soviet tanks rolled into Afghanistan. He informed me that Ahmad Zahir's father, Abdul Zahir, had been a doctor at the court of King Zahir Shah.

Two years after separating from his wife, Zahir had become friendly with an Egyptian woman in Hamburg called Marwah who was ten years older than him and worked as a carer for elderly people. "She came to see me at my home on Sundays. She was a warm person who cared for me but my relationship with her was more by way of overcoming the grief of the separation from my wife than a whole-hearted attempt to start all over again."

The parents and brothers of Zahir's estranged wife lived in California. Her brothers ran a limousine hire business and were doing well. Zahir was extremely hard up when he arrived in Hamburg, which was one of the reasons for his separation from his wife. He saw his children only once a month but paid his wife half his salary for their upkeep. He was living in a rented flat but sublet one of the rooms in the flat to help make ends meet. I asked Zahir if he planned to practice medicine in Germany. "It's a tall order," he replied, "because five years have passed since I last practiced medicine, in Kabul." The separation from his wife and children had broken his resolve to study again and pass the necessary exams in Germany. He had spent the last five years learning German but still didn't feel confident in his use of this second language.

Zahir wore Afghan clothes only at home and didn't go out in his ethnic gear even to the local shops. He had once gone to a local supermarket in his home clothes and a group of children playing in the street had mockingly shouted "schlafanzug, schlafanzug", which means jim-jams, and he could never bring himself to venture out in Afghan clothes again. I must say that Zahir was very kind to me while I was living in his rented flat, telling me that I should feel free to use anything there at all.

One day I came home in the evening and switched on the TV. There was a news report about bloodshed in Kashmir after the Mirwaiz (a Muslim Grand Preacher) was killed. The site of the bloodshed wasn't that far from my home in Srinagar. I tried desperately to call my parents but it was impossible to get through to them since telecommunications were disrupted in Kashmir. When I finally got through two days later it turned out to be a wrong number. The person who picked up the phone was living in another neighbourhood but obligingly offered to go to my parents' home and give them my message of concern. It wasn't until a week later that I managed to speak to them but they told me that someone had come to their home and delivered my message. All of them were safe and sound except a close relative who had been shot several times and was being treated in hospital. I felt bereft that so many people lost their lives when paramilitary soldiers shot the protestors carrying the Mirwaiz's body.

Zahir spent most of his time at work and did his household chores at weekends. He cleaned his flat on Saturdays and did the grocery shopping on Sundays. He showed me a supermarket where he bought his groceries, explaining that it was cheaper than other supermarkets. I didn't realise at the time that a few pfennigs difference in the price of various items meant a substantial different in the total price of a shopping basket. My first trip to a supermarket in Germany was mind-blowing. I couldn't decide what to buy from the sheer variety of fruit and vegetables displayed on the shelves. Some kinds of fruit and veg appeared exotic to me. I hadn't seen a kiwi fruit, sharon fruit or a custard apple (known as "sharifa" in India) before and wasn't at all sure how they were eaten. I was even baffled to see apples without the slightest blemish on supermarket shelves in Hamburg. Although Kashmir is well-known for growing apples, you couldn't find such perfect-looking apples in the entire valley. Sharif usually brought apples from his orchard in Hamburg to Kashmir but my cousin thought their quality was inferior to those from his own orchard. The fruits on the shelves of Hamburg supermarkets came from many countries – people in Europe were lucky to be treated to such a wide variety of fruit from all over the world. For me as a relative newcomer, walking in the aisles of a supermarket was like wandering through the Garden of Eden.

Zahir cooked Afghan food on Sundays and always saved a portion for me. I sometimes asked a friend or acquaintance from Kashmir who was visiting Hamburg to have dinner at my home and ordered food from the Afghan restaurant near the Freihafen. The restaurant had a clay oven to grill lamb and chicken and they served the grilled meat on a big round Afghan flatbread with fresh leaves of mint. It was too big a portion for one person but it was inexpensive. Since I was Sharif's guest, the restaurant owner didn't want to accept any money from me when I ordered food from him but I always insisted that he accept payment or I wouldn't order any food from him again. It was a great relief to finally let my friends and acquaintances know where I lived in Hamburg and invite them to my home for dinner.

One day I went to the home of a businessman from Kashmir who lived in Rothenbaumchaussee. The neighbourhood boasted elegant-looking houses and the streets were crowded with people. My host informed me that there was a tennis stadium in the area and the crowd I saw was coming out of the stadium after seeing a match. I asked him about the very long name of his street. He said it derived from a red tree ('Rothenbaum' in German) which once stood near there. He was about to cook Kashmiri food and I watched how he mixed spices to prepare the dishes, thinking it was time for me to learn how to cook food from my homeland. As I was walking down Rothenbaumchaussee to go home late at night, I saw a convertible car halted at a traffic light with a man at the wheel caressing a fair-haired woman in his arms. I could not deny feelings of loneliness during my walk home.

Zahir's wife came to collect her children from his home on a Sunday afternoon. She had blonde streaks in her hair and wore fashionable boots. I imagined she would ignore Zahir's girlfriend, Marwah, but they engaged in small talk. In fact it was Zahir who didn't greet his wife. It was heartbreaking for him not to see his children for weeks on end. Zahir had sacrificed everything on his journey from Kabul to Hamburg, never imagining that his wife might separate from him. He told me that sometimes he wished that he could turn back the clock and never attempt such a journey.

I accompanied Zahir to a big mosque in Hamburg that he occasionally visited. Many Pakistani men gathered there to hear guest speakers. Among the congregation I recognised a Kebab-shop owner from the Reeperbahn. He was with his daughter, who was probably 5 or 6 years old. A German professor who had converted to Islam was a guest of honour. Zahir told me that the Pakistani congregation was divided into two camps – those who supported the People's Party, which had been removed from power in a coup, and those who supported Zia-ul-Haq, the General responsible for their defeat. The guest speaker that day appealed to the congregation to show unity despite their opposing political views. Zahir, I noticed, wasn't keen to engage in conversation with any of the factions there.

As spring turned into summer in1990, the people of Hamburg began to be gripped by football fever. The World Cup tournament in Italy was the last time that Germany played as a divided country, East and West. The excitement was palpable in Hamburg as West Germany reached the Finals and it turned out to be a night of fireworks when the team triumphantly beat Argentina. A few weeks later, I met a football fan from Kashmir who was travelling to Rome to visit the stadium where the Finals were played and kick a football on the pitch that he regarded as sacred.

I joined a language school in Hamburg to learn German, having already attended a basic course at the University of Kashmir. "Why do you want to learn German?" the tutor in Kashmir asked me. "Because I want to read German literature," I replied. This made him smile because that was well beyond the scope of an elementary course. My cousin called me into his office one day to test my knowledge of the new language and asked me to name various things in the office in German even though he didn't speak the language. This was still the case a few months later when the two of us happened to be sitting in a fast food restaurant in Delhi. My cousin noticed that a Punjabi man sitting at an adjacent table was pestering two German women at the next table and asked me to tell the women not to mind him because he was a madman. I thought it too risky a proposition and kept quiet.

Sharif knew that I had attended a course in Kashmir to learn German. One morning he gave me a copy of the newspaper, *Die Zeit*, and asked me to read a paragraph from it. He wanted to ascertain the level of my German from my reading alone and didn't ask me to translate it. I was glad that he didn't because there were so many unfamiliar words in the newspaper report that its meaning was over my head.

Zahir was working for an Iranian businessman in Freihafen and spoke Farsi with his employer. His level of German was intermediate, which wasn't good enough for him to pass a medical exam to get back into his own profession. However, his children went to school in Hamburg and had a good comprehension of German. Perhaps his only consolation was the belief that his children would not suffer from the same limitations that he experienced in Germany.

I had met Zahir's Iranian employer once in Sharif's office. He was tall and lean, with a full head of grey hair. He wore a long coat and a hat and didn't come across as Iranian to me. Faiz told me that he had the reputation of being a flamboyant man. But he took a long time to pay his suppliers. Sometimes he borrowed money from Sharif to pay them but didn't repay that loan either on time. Zahir knew that his boss frequented a gambling casino, preferring to lose his money at roulette rather than pay his suppliers on time. According to Zahir, his boss wasn't particularly fond of the Afghan people, despite the fact that they spoke the same language.

Knowing his medical background, the Afghans who visited Sharif's office usually asked Zahir for advice if they weren't feeling well. One of his friends from Kabul worked in a pharmacy in Hamburg and he was able to get medicine for them from this contact. Zahir was called to give first aid if any Afghan or Iranian man working in the warehouses in Freihafen hurt himself. Perhaps his boss reckoned that Zahir's medical knowledge would come in useful when he offered him the bookkeeping job. Zahir had actually worked in a warehouse in Hamburg before and knew it was hard work to pack and unpack heavy goods so he had sympathy with his co-workers in Freihafen.

Zahir's separation from his wife and children weighed heavily on him that he seemed to me to be a broken man. He had sought refuge from the war in Afghanistan but his freedom had cost him his marriage, which caused him deep anguish. He believed that his wife wouldn't have separated from him in Kabul for fear of the animosity it would have caused between her own family and her husband's family. Although his wife came from another tribe, he felt that he would have received a favourable decision from a Jirga – a tribal council – if his case had reached them.

On a Sunday morning, I accompanied Zahir to the Fischmarkt, a flea-market along the Elbe near the port of Hamburg. Although it was very early, the market was already teeming with people. "I spent many Sundays here after my marriage broke up", he told me. "The bustle reminded me of

the markets in Kabul. I even found live chickens for sale here."
The images of the St Pauli terminal with its clock tower and
patina domes had persisted in my mind's eye since my first visit
to Hamburg two years earlier. You could see a jumble of iron
cranes behind the big stone building, and huge cruise liners
and ships laden with sea-containers passing by. In the early
evening, the bright lights of the harbour gave the impression
of enormous commercial activity. This greatly impressed me.
Until I visited Hamburg, I had never been to a port city and
had only read about such places (and their main exports) in
school textbooks.

Many years after visiting Hamburg, I took part in
one of the London Walks around Whitechapel and met an
American tourist who had travelled from Hamburg to visit
London. He recounted the story of a ship, the SS St Louis,
that had set sail from Hamburg in 1939 with 900 Jews, many
of them children, bound for Cuba to escape the Nazis. The
ship was turned away, firstly from Havana and then from
Florida, and forced to return to Europe. European countries
like Britain, the Netherlands, Belgium and France took some
of its passengers but 250 men, women and children were
refused sanctuary and subsequently killed by the Nazis. His
own parents, he told me, had fled Europe and made it to
America, but he felt distraught whenever he thought about
the fate of the passengers on board the SS St Louis after it was
turned away from America, the country of his birth.

Their journey had been a matter of life or death.

It formed a troubling, timeless continuum with the striving of my friends in Hamburg for a better life and today's afflicted refugees in their quest for survival.

An Evening by the Neckar

The association of Heidelberg with printing presses has left an indelible impression on my memory ever since my adolescence. There were only two professions that, as a child, I thought were worth pursuing – a printer and a bookbinder. In fact, there was a very fortunate man in our neighbourhood in Srinagar who was both a printer and a bookbinder. I imagined a bookbinder to be a kind of alchemist who turns base metal into gold since he turned a set of used school textbooks at the beginning of each academic year into a brand new set for the students that bought them second-hand. In fact, the few bookbinders in Srinagar became very surly at the end of the school year because they were too much in demand.

When a bookbinder failed to return my middle sister's books for several days, my mother asked my eldest uncle to have a word with the printer since he was the only one in our family capable of raising his voice in dealing with a crusty bookbinder. To everyone's surprise, he came back with the books the same day.

I would stop at a bookbinder's shop near my school and watch him press the books in a cast-iron machine. He trimmed the books with a giant guillotine and collected the shredded edges in hessian sacks to be sold as packaging for fragile goods. The bookbinder used colourful patterned paper for the covering of the textbooks and usually used one pattern for a whole set so that it was easy to identify the owner of a textbook in a classroom by the design of its cover. He made the paste for books in his shop by mixing wheat flour with starch.

The local newspapers had started to publish their Sunday supplements in colour and heralded themselves as the owners of offset printing presses. I couldn't figure out the meaning of the word 'offset' used in conjunction with the phrase 'printing press' – I only saw a colour printing press from a distance when the door of a neighbouring metal shed that housed one was ajar. However, I could see a typesetter working with his tools at a shop of the printer who was also a bookbinder. But proofreading wasn't accorded any importance and no one paid much attention to typographical errors. There was just one publisher in our town, and he had published only a handful of books over many years. He was principally a bookseller and his main business was selling the books of publishers from Delhi and other big cities. One day I removed the dust jacket of one of his books and saw that the word Kashmir, written on its spine in gold ink, was misspelt. But obviously it didn't matter because people still talked highly of the work of our sole publisher.

Our school textbooks were mostly in paperback form and bookbinders sewed their pages together by making holes with a spike and then passing a thin but strong string through them before placing pieces of millboard at the front and back and covering the spine with Buckram cloth. Some of the textbooks didn't have enough margins to allow for such sewing. So the first few letters of the words at the beginning of each line would be covered when these books were held wide open. I had handed my album of precious postage stamps to the bookbinder and, while trimming the edges, his guillotine had chopped off the borders of my stamps affixed to the margins. I sobbed when I saw what he'd done.

Although I had heard about the printing presses made in Heidelberg when I was growing up in Kashmir, it wasn't until I moved to London that I saw one with my own eyes. I ran errands on my bike for a stationer in northwest London and sometimes carried a box of brown parcel tape on its rack to a printer in the neighbourhood. He had a Heidelberg press in one corner and told me that he had been using it for more than 40 years and it was still working smoothly.

I decided to visit a friend who lived near Heidelberg in 2010. Although tourism plays an important part in the economy of Heidelberg it is considered in some contemporary travel guides to be an underrated tourist destination. I applied for a visa at the German embassy in London. I had been to this embassy in Belgravia many years earlier, accompanying a family friend from Kashmir who was visiting London and wanted to visit Continental Europe. The visa officer refused to issue a visa for my friend and told him that he would have to apply for it in his country of origin. I tried to plead on his behalf but the officer insisted that his *no* meant *no*.

I deposited my passport in the morning and came back in the afternoon to collect it. The official at the counter told me there was a problem and asked me if I had overstayed in Germany during my previous visit. I told him that I had visited Germany many times but never stayed in the country beyond the time validated by my visa. He asked me to wait for a few minutes to verify it and went into his office at the back. When he returned shortly afterwards, he apologized and explained that there was someone else by the same name but from a different country who had outstayed his welcome in Germany, and without further ado he handed me my passport with a visa stamped on it.

As my plane circled around the high-rise building in the centre of Frankfurt am Main before landing, the lights on the ground appeared blindingly bright. I would have liked to take a train from the airport to Heidelberg but the friend I was visiting had come to pick me up in his own car. He lived in a small town near Heidelberg. A section of the motorway was being resurfaced with new concrete and my friend proudly declared, "This is Germany – they don't use tarmac here." It took him less than an hour to cover the distance of 50 miles from Frankfurt to Heidelberg, roughly the same time it had taken me that morning to cover a distance of 15 miles from my home to Heathrow Airport. But it never thrills me to travel on a motorway and I tend to prefer the back roads on which motorists have to curb their speed.

I had booked accommodation in a hotel that was just a short distance from the city centre. The hotel is perched along the river Neckar in a peaceful location between a footbridge and a dual carriageway bridge. Looking through the window of my room, I saw a lock near the footbridge and realised that the Neckar is canalized as it passes through Heidelberg. There is a magnificent gorge on the other side and the landscape is very picturesque. The restaurant in the hotel overlooks the river and in the morning I saw many barges going up and downriver, suggesting much industrial activity in the region.

I left the hotel in the morning for a stroll along the Neckar. Wanting to cross the road outside the hotel, I looked up at the traffic light and saw the name 'Iqbal-Ufer' on a signboard above it. I had heard about this road sign from someone who taught German at Kashmir University but never thought that I would stumble upon it on my second day in Heidelberg right outside the hotel where I was staying. The road along Neckar was named after a poet of our sub-continent, Allama Iqbal. My mother had perhaps named me after him, since Allama Iqbal's ancestors hailed from Kashmir. An American in London once asked me if my name was the same as that of the anti-war activist, Eqbal Ahmed.

I remembered having read a poem, 'An Evening by the Neckar', by Allama Iqbal when I was a student. The poet evokes a moon that, like Baudelaire's *lune*, is dying in swoons.

Allama Iqbal had lived in Heidelberg as a student for a few years at the beginning of the last century. Heidelberg is also the university town where Sigmund Romberg's Student Prince arrives from a fictitious kingdom to be properly educated. There is also a prison in Heidelberg in which students were locked up for being unruly.

The walk along Iqbal-Ufer took me to Heidelberg's landmark bridge made of red sandstone and a walk over this bridge leads to a road called Philosopher's Way. After catching views of the river and the castle, it is easy to understand why Heidelberg is known as a romantic city.

Like any other university town, Heidelberg is an ideal place for cyclists. I saw men and women riding bikes with trailers for kids attached, reminding me of a London newspaper that routinely advertised German-made commuter bikes. The banks of the river Neckar provide a fine scenic route for cyclists. While riding a bike in London, on the other hand, I am fearful of the concrete mixers on the roads, some of which belong to the Heidelberg Cement Group.

I saw many Arab guests having breakfast in the restaurant of the hotel where I was staying, some of whom looked rather unwell. A few of them spoke to the waitress in Arabic. Lamia was from Morocco and had worked in this hotel for seven years. She told me that there was a university hospital on the other side of the river and most of the Arabs staying in the hotel came to Heidelberg for treatment there. The president of an Arab country was currently undergoing surgery in this hospital.

My host in Heidelberg, Jehangir, was a friend from my old neighbourhood in Srinagar. My acquaintance with him began in my childhood when I saw him at his uncle's home in our neighbourhood. He had moved to Germany in the mid-1980s after marrying a German woman who was visiting Kashmir for a few weeks. He had worked his way up in a fast food restaurant chain, joining the ranks of its higher management, and had set up his own business in Heidelberg a few years ago. It was a long journey, though, from his arrival in Germany as a newlywed having to learn a new language and a new culture. He now spoke Kashmiri interspersed with German words, with the result that some of his relatives in Kashmir mistakenly believed that he spoke a higher form of the Kashmiri language. Jehangir's own family members in Srinagar had become familiar with odd German words and sometimes confounded others by using them.

When I last met Jehangir in Srinagar, we went to Cafe de Linz for tea. There was a group of men sitting at a table next to ours and one of them remarked to the others that Asians living in London were despised by their neighbours for hanging their washing from windows. Jehangir got up and asked this person if he had ever been to London. The man said no. Jehangir had himself visited London recently and told the man that he disagreed with him. There was a chat-show host among the group who, aware they were being challenged, asked Jehangir to sit with them and tell him more about his trip to London. I was taken aback by Jehangir's outpouring.

I thought it impolite of him to pose such a direct question to a stranger in a coffee-shop. He told me later that he had learnt from his German friends to ask direct questions rather than going through a courteous rigmarole.

Jehangir had been accepted into the Heidelberg milieu by virtue of his marriage to a woman from a small town in the state of Baden-Württemberg. His mother has once advised me against two things: taking up a job in Europe or America and marrying a foreign woman. She knew very well that the sons of our Kashmiri soil would never return once they settled down with a spouse and employment overseas.

We drove up a hill in the evening for dinner with Dorothy, a friend of Jehangir whose son acted as his lawyer for his commercial dealings. He parked his car on a steep slope and we walked up a garden path to reach Dorothy's home, which turned out to be an idyllic-looking cottage. Dorothy, an amiable and sociable woman, had invited a few other people for dinner that evening. Conversation at the dinner table mostly revolved around local issues. Jehangir had once told me that his German friends usually confided in him because they didn't consider him to be an outsider. I thought it was more likely due to his friendliness, which was reciprocated by his friends and his wife's relatives in Germany.

Jehangir had worked in the tourist industry in Kashmir and one of his uncles had taught him the rules of hospitality. The home of his uncle was an open house and he usually invited a lot of people to his home, from policemen to clergymen.

He told his nephew that knowing one person is like knowing the whole world and that acquaintances were necessary if you were working in the tourist trade in Kashmir because you never knew whose help you were going to need to survive in a very seasonal business. Jehangir drove his uncle to various tourist locations in Kashmir and they came to be known as a duo among the businessmen in Srinagar. The habits of his uncle had rubbed off on Jehangir who often invited his lawyer, accountant and other such people to his home in Germany. I was quite surprised to learn that a Heidelberg policeman was one of his family friends.

Dorothy was a fine cook and had prepared a lot of food for her guests. The other people at the dinner party, all from Heidelberg, were related to her. But they all seemed to know Jehangir and talked to him about his business and other matters.

Jehangir was friends with a mayor of one of the towns in Baden-Württemberg. He had once invited the mayor on a vacation to London and I had met him at the hotel where they stayed. When a receptionist at the hotel asked Jehangir to show an ID at the check-in, he told her jokingly that he should be exempted from such formalities because he was accompanied by a VIP. Jehangir wanted me to meet his friend again in Heidelberg and rang his office. He spoke to his secretary and after some small talk left a message for her boss inviting him to meet us for dinner in a restaurant in town.

It was a German restaurant and almost empty when we arrived early that evening. The mayor arrived on time and the restaurant began to fill slowly. He was happy to see us both and remarked, "Don't expect the same quick service in a Heidelberg restaurant as the one where we ate in London." The mayor belonged to the opposition party and Jehangir said knowingly that he had voted for the opposition party in the last election. As we were leaving the restaurant, I saw police cars parked outside and some of the officers were on the point of entering the restaurant. I asked the mayor what the police were doing there since it was perfectly peaceful inside the restaurant. He explained that the police wanted to check if there was anyone working in the restaurant kitchen who had overstayed in Germany. "I hope not," he said. " It would be politically embarrassing for me if they arrest some errant dishwasher because I'm one of the patrons of this restaurant."

Jehangir was living in Leimen, a small town lying a few miles south of Heidelberg. He liked to associate his hometown with one of its notable citizens if someone hadn't heard its name. It was, he stated, the birthplace of the famous tennis player, Boris Becker. Jehangir also mentioned that Steffi Graff hailed from another small town in his home state of Baden-Württemberg. I remembered once meeting Jehangir at a wedding reception in London when he told the guests there that he ran a business in a big town in Germany. It made me smile because Heidelberg's population was not much more than 150,000.

Three days after arriving in Heidelberg, Jehangir drove me to his home in Leimen. He stopped at a bank on the way and the manager offered us a coffee. Jehangir had lived in the same town ever since he arrived in Germany 25 years ago. As he drove through the town, he stopped at a few places for small talk with his neighbours and told me that he enjoyed the same bond with people living in Leimen as he had with the residents of his old neighbourhood in Srinagar.

Jehangir seemed to know most of the people living in his quiet cul-de-sac. One of his elderly neighbours was fixing a car in a garage opposite his house. Jehangir asked him if he needed help and invited him to pop into his home. He poured a drink for him and wished him good health. He told me later that he considered it his duty to look after the elderly people in his street. In fact, Jehangir's mother-in-law was living on her own a few doors down the road and he went to see her every day.

He took me around to see her. 'Mamma', as he was fond of calling her, was sitting in an armchair when he opened the door of her flat, to which he had a key. She could only see partially and needed help with household chores. Jehangir liked to take her dog for a walk in the evening. I wanted to stretch my legs and was happy to join him on this daily walk.

We passed a few rows of houses until we reached a desolate open area. I asked Jehangir if he was ever scared of walking alone in the evening around there. "If you walk with a dog" he said, "you would scare others more than some crazy people scaring you." A few minutes later, I saw a figure at a distance. I thought at first that it was a scarecrow but then I saw it was a man, walking towards us with a dog trailing behind. When he reached us I heard him muttering "Ausländer raus" – Foreigners Out. Jehangir advised me not to pay any attention because he must be crazy to talk to himself. But I could see Jehangir was a little embarrassed by this incident.

I accompanied Jehangir the next day as he drove around Heidelberg on various business appointments. He was meeting his accountant in the morning. The accountant's office was very chic – the kind of office usually occupied by architects in London. The filing drawers were fitted on the wall. Jehangir's grey-haired accountant was perhaps a few years older than the retirement age for men. Everyone in his office seemed to know Jehangir and greeted him. "I don't like the idea of changing my accountant, lawyer or doctor," he told me. "I've always been a loyal client."

The life of every German resident is regulated by bureaucracy. Although Jehangir disliked this bureaucracy, he followed all the regulations applied to running a business in Baden-Württemberg. He reminisced about the fly-by-night nature of many tourist businesses in Kashmir in the 1980s, admitting that he couldn't forgive himself for having working as a tout during that time. "I can't tell a lie even in jest since I moved to Leiman," he told me. "I don't like to cut corners either when it comes to running my own business in Heidelberg. Efficiency is important." This reminded me of the occasion when a German guest signed a document at our hotel desk in London using his fountain pen. He flipped the pen round and it became a rubber stamp. I told him it was a clever piece of design. 'What do you expect?' he replied. "I am a bloody German."

Jehangir liked his coffee ritual in the morning and took me to his favourite cafe in Heidelberg, opposite his office in the centre of town. Since he also ran a fast food (Schnellimbiss) restaurant next door to the coffee-shop, they offered him a coffee at a special price. He could watch people relishing a Currywurst outside his fast food restaurant while having his Americano. Jehangir was very particular about keeping the forecourt of his restaurant tidy and there were instructions displayed on the wall in the restaurant kitchen for the staff about how to separate the waste for recycling. He had delegated all day-to-day tasks to his staff. "I wouldn't have time for other business if I get involved in ordering supplies for my restaurant and making the timetable for the staff. I've entrusted those responsibilities to someone who manages the restaurant for me." She was working under him when he was the Area Manager of a fast food chain and chose to work for him when he opened his own restaurant.

I toured the town with Jehangir while he was checking the menus of similar restaurants to gauge his competition. "The rent I pay for the restaurant is very high but it's still a profitable business for me because of its location. I received a thorough training in gastronomy while working for a restaurant chain that was well known for the training of its staff. I'm also fond of eating out and always look for ideas to improve my fast food business. To be successful in business," he added, "you have to like what you do."

Jehangir met a few other owners of businesses in Heidelberg for lunch in an Italian restaurant five days a week. We were greeted by Giovanni, who owned the restaurant, where a long table was reserved for local business people every day around noon. Giovanni was like a confidant and knew much about the members of this group. Sometimes they left messages with him for each other. It was an informal meeting place and the members of the group benefited by exchanging their ideas.

It was two decades since Jehangir's arrival in Germany. He had prospered through hard graft and now he took it easy and enjoyed being the owner of two or three businesses. He had his own private office in the centre of town, which he used for a short period during the course of his day. One of the rooms on his office floor was used by his German business partner, Dietmar. They were more like friends than business associates. He often met Dietmar and his family for dinner in a brasserie in the town. It was an atmospheric place, so busy that it was difficult to find a free table there in the evening. When we arrived at the restaurant, Dietmar was already there with his wife and asked a waitress for two more chairs to be placed at his small table.

Dietmar was chatting to a couple who were eating at a nearby table. When they left, I asked him if he knew them. He said that he had never met them before but had struck up a conversation with them while waiting for us. He found the modern experience of connecting with people who are far away while ignoring those sitting next to us very alienating. Dietmar said that although he used all the modern gadgets he wasn't a big fan of technology. He preferred to socialize in the evenings and didn't discuss any business-related matters with Jehangir. The brasserie was buzzing with laughter, which was why, Dietmar explained, it was one of his favourite haunts.

Heidelberg is a student town and Jehangir employed quite a few students in his fast food restaurants. One of them was managed by a student called Hashmat, who was from Sialkot in Pakistan. He had lived in Frankfurt for a few years before moving to Heidelberg. He ran his own business in Frankfurt but had lost money and incurred debts. He sighed as he showed me pictures of his warehouse brimming with leather goods like biker trousers, jackets and handbags. Hashmat's family produced the leather goods in Sialkot and he had opened a branch in Frankfurt for their own products to have direct access to the EU market.

"It's tough for Hashmat to pay off his debts," Jehangir told me, "even though he's working as a restaurant manager and earns a fair wage. I have sympathy for him because I've known adversity myself, when I was living in Kashmir. I met him in Frankfurt and asked him to manage one of my restaurants in Heidelberg." Hashmat told me that his sister and her husband lived in Whitechapel in London and owned a few shops there. He gave me the name of one of their shops and asked me to look in if I happened to be visiting the East End.

It's a cold world out there for immigrants in Europe in the second decade of the third millennium. Jehangir realised that migration had become a defining issue at the beginning of this century. "I consider Leiman to be my home-town. As for my ancestral home in Srinagar, it's now my *zweite heimat* – my second home. But I understand the predicaments of people who've arrived recently in Germany and I know how indifferent natives can be to outsiders. They are men without women and it's a surreal experience to find oneself surrounded by beautiful women and yet be all alone. Take Hashmat. He's never had a relationship with a woman since he came to live in Germany ten years ago and he's not sure if he can ever find love in the supposedly romantic city of Heidelberg. Still, Hashmat is bearing his sorrows lightly and seems more concerned about paying off his debts than finding a soul mate."

Jehangir also spoke about his wife. "I'm very grateful to her. She helped me learn a new language and a new culture when I moved to Germany. We started a family soon, when I was in my early twenties. My wife didn't work after giving birth and proved to be an anchor for my life in Baden-Württemberg. I think highly of Swabian women and my wife is a real home-maker."

I asked Jehangir whether he knew anyone from Srinagar in Heidelberg but he wasn't sure if there was anyone else from Kashmir currently living there. "I knew just one person from Lake Dal in Kashmir. He lived with his German wife in Frankfurt. One day I heard that the man had been arrested for beating his wife. Since then I didn't want to know him. I can't understand how a man could beat up his other half. I once met some men from Srinagar in Heidelberg who were travelling to Baden-Baden to gamble in the casino and I thought it was outrageous that anyone from Kashmir would travel to Germany just to gamble."

On my last day in Heidelberg, I asked Jehangir to park his car somewhere and join me for a stroll through Heidelberg's Old Town. We left the hotel and passed a glass cube of a building that houses Print Media Academy. It features a huge stainless sculpture in the shape of a horse, symbolising the workhorse that is a Heidelberg printing press. Jehangir told me that there is a scarlet auditorium in the basement of the building surrounded by water, thereby representing two elements of offset printing – ink and water. On the way to the Old Town, he showed me the hospital where his wife had given birth to his last-born child. He said it was nice to go there in December because of the Christmas market and he visited every year.

We drifted into the alleyways of the Old Town and came upon an empty space with a sign stating that a synagogue stood at that site until 10th November 1938. I recognized the date of *Kristallnacht*, when the Nazis attacked Jewish shops and torched synagogues in Germany. There were twelve sandstone cubes built on the site to represent the twelve Jewish tribes.

It is a stark and poignant reminder of what could happen if the current resurgence of nationalism in our world gains strength.

Mannheim's Little Istanbul

The city of Mannheim is located about 11 miles from Heidelberg at the confluence of the Neckar and the Rhine rivers. Although its population was less than 300,000 when I first visited it in 2010, the city felt much bigger than Heidelberg which has half that number of inhabitants. However, unlike its neighbouring city, whose reputation is built on printing presses and a medieval university, Mannheim is the city in which the first ever motorcar was built by Karl Benz. It was launched on New Year's Eve, 1879. Mannheim is also the place where another Karl – Drais – invented the prototype of a bicycle six decades earlier. It was called a running machine and nicknamed a 'dandy horse'. These days, many cyclists prefer to call their bike an iron horse since dandyism has gone out of fashion.

There was only one Mercedes Benz car in our town in Kashmir. It belonged to a Moulvi – a preacher – who was also a politician and it was usually borrowed for weddings by his relatives to carry a bridegroom with much razzmatazz to the bride's home. I knew this car existed though I'd never seen it on the road. But a garage owner in Srinagar declared his pride in servicing Mercedes cars by advertising it on his signboard in big letters. It was difficult to pronounce the name of this German-made car and many people in Srinagar called it a 'Mercerie' as if it were a French haberdasher's favourite vehicle. I was once told that Mercedes was the name of the daughter of one of the earlier owners of the car company that manufactured it and it meant 'godsend' in Spanish. I thought it an apt name since our preacher certainly considered his German car to be a heavenly gift.

I was standing at a street corner in the old town of Srinagar when a car ran into a horse-drawn cart. The driver of the car was enraged. He got out of his car and shouted at the horse-and-cart man, demanding to know whether he thought he was driving a Mercedes rather than a cart. It was meant as a belittling insult. During my childhood, there was a businessman from Srinagar who had travelled to Germany and when people asked him what was the most unusual thing he had seen in the country he told them it was Mercedes cars being used as taxis. The second unusual thing he mentioned was that he didn't see any rubbish dumped in open spaces as was the case in his own backyard. His neighbours found his second observation more bizarre than the first.

On my first visit to Germany, I saw a Mercedes in the forecourt of a garage with its bonnet open while a mechanic was having a look inside. The engine and other parts were so neatly and tightly packed that I thought my father's Ambassador car with its metal casing was hollow in comparison. Some people like to call it a Merc, whereas others call it a Benz. I once worked in London with a man from the Caribbean who fancied a woman from the West Indies. He was so surprised when he saw another suitor of the lady he admired driving a Mercedes car that he broke into Janis Joplin's song, "Oh Lord, won't you buy me a Mercedes Benz?"

Jehangir, the friend I was visiting in Leiman, lived not far away from his cousin Zulifkar in Mannheim and he drove me there to see him as I had known him in Kashmir. His family had fallen on hard times before the cousins were born. The grown-up Jehangir had brought his cousin over to Germany so he could help support his family. Jehangir had initially employed Zulifkar and then helped him to set up his own business. So Zulifkar was immensely grateful to his cousin for being such a guardian angel.

I had last met Zulifkar in the early 1990s when he was struggling to keep his head above water by selling Kashmir shawls at a market stall in New Delhi. I happened to visit the market and he invited me for a cup of tea at his stall. He stood upright in front of this stall from morning till evening, trying to persuade passers-by to buy a shawl but managing to sell only a few each day. We sat on a white sheet on the ground to have tea and he sprang up every time he saw a foreign tourist walking by. He tried even harder with tourists, attempting to sell his shawls as souvenirs of Kashmir. Zulifkar confided in me that sometimes he wished he sold groceries instead so that he didn't have to beg potential customers to buy his merchandise.

I asked Zulifkar why it was it so hard to sell shawls from Kashmir when the region was renowned for producing fine textiles. He told me it was a tough trade partly because of the justified reputation of Kashmiri shawl merchants as astute salesmen. "They usually weigh up a prospective buyer before telling them the price of a shawl. If they price a shawl at 15,000 rupees they might sell it for 1,500 after haggling with the customer and still make a small profit." I found it baffling that a vendor could make a profit on a commodity sold at one tenth of the marked price. "Some of the shawl sellers from Kashmir," he added, "when they visit the homes of prospective clients in Mumbai or Delhi, they'll ask for permission to pray right there in the middle of showing them their wares so that buyers will assume the shawl seller is an honest, God-fearing man." This rang true. I remembered reading VS Naipaul's account of his encounter with a shawl merchant around the Lake Dal area who offered a prayer during the transaction.

It is often considered a risky thing to buy a shawl from an itinerant Kashmiri salesman. These salesmen liked to brag when they gathered at a wedding or a funeral in Srinagar about how they persuaded an unwilling client to buy a shawl from them. Someone would boast how his grandfather had sold a shawl to Bollywood legend, Raj Kapoor, and another would tell what it meant for his uncle to sell a shawl to a client in Calcutta's upmarket Chowringhee Lane. "You know something," said Zulifkar, "if a top shawl merchant from the time of the Raj were to return from the grave, he would find it difficult to sell a single shawl because there are so many other salesmen around."

It wasn't Zulifkar's family business to sell shawls so he found it difficult to compete with the vendors whose grandfathers had been in the business for years and therefore knew all the tricks of the trade. Older vendors could speak Bengali and Marathi and were so familiar with the habits and tastes of the people living in various regions of India that they knew, for instance, that it was easier to sell a shawl to a Punjabi than a Gujrati woman. Many shawl vendors offered their wares on credit to Bengali housewives and collected money from them in instalments. They sold the shawls at the beginning of winter in Calcutta and collected payment from Bengali families periodically until returning to Kashmir in the spring.

A few vendors pretended to be still living in Calcutta after they returned to Kashmir and wore light clothes for a week or two even though it was cold in Kashmir in early spring. Some of them even sported loincloths and sandals. But their pretence would usually end in a fortnight or so. The shawl vendors paid their suppliers when they returned from Calcutta. A few tenacious vendors stayed in Bengal until the beginning of summer to collect payment from their clients. But if someone stayed through the summer, his relative in Srinagar guessed that the man had found a spouse there and was hiding his relationship from his friends and family. Rumours about such a person would run and run in Srinagar and if a man was unable to find a woman to marry in Kashmir, his relatives would tease him by saying that they could always find a woman for him in Bengal.

The men who sold shawls from Kashmir have become proverbial magicians in Bengali and Punjabi folklore and most of the people know that their prices are fantastical. Zulifkar said that no one would buy a shawl from him if his prices were fixed. And it was impossible for him to negotiate with two customers bargaining at the same time. While I was having tea at his stall, a group of women who were either relatives or friends started bargaining with him over the price of an inexpensive shawl. Zulifkar was flustered and refused to lower the price further in hope they would move on to another stall. "That's why," he told me, "some of the shawl vendors hire an assistant – to deal with such awkward 'special' customers."

Zulifkar had seen the fortunes of other families living in his neighbourhood in Srinagar change since his childhood and was keen to do something to improve his own family circumstances. Although he was taking risks in business he didn't exactly know how to escape the daily grind of selling shawls at a market stall in Delhi. His cousin had asked Zulifkar to work for him in Heidelberg a few months after I met him in New Delhi. He had brought a selection of shawls with him in his suitcase when he travelled to Germany but had realised very soon that he wasn't going to make it as a shawl vendor in Baden-Württemberg, preferring rather to work at two jobs a day for however long it took until he was able to set up his own business in Mannheim.

Two jobs a day had taken its toll on Zulifkar. I remembered him as an athletic but nervy kind of person when I met him in New Delhi. He had put on weight since I last saw him. He told me that he had eaten fast food for a decade while rushing from one job to another. "But since I got married a few years ago, I mostly eat at home now and find it difficult to get into shape again." However, he seemed to have accepted this as the price for improving the lives of his family in Srinagar.

"For many years," he told me, "I worked for 16 hours a day and had no time for socialising. I'd get up at 5 am, leave home at 6 o'clock and return home at midnight. I was managing a restaurant for Jehangir in Heidelberg and then commuted to Mannheim to work for a haulier." He'd eaten a lot of unhealthy food during those years, which accounted for his considerable weight gain. However, he didn't lament having become unfit but was grateful that he had the opportunity to work long hours. "There are a lot of people like me living in Mannheim and other parts of Germany who hold down two jobs to support ourselves and our parents and siblings in other countries."

Since Zulifkar had opened his own pizza restaurant, his friends and relatives admired him more for his perseverance than his acumen. "Some of them envy me because I'm doing well." But Jehangir was proud of his cousin for finally opening his own business in Germany and taking care of his family in Kashmir. He had got married in Kashmir three years ago and had a two-year-old son. Zulifkar was only a year younger than Jehangir, who had grown-up children. He told me that his grandfather had become a great-grandfather at 48. Zulifkar made sacrifices in life for the sake of his parents and siblings.

"Some of our wealthier relatives didn't invite us to their weddings when we were struggling in Srinagar. But now many distant relatives often come to visit my mother. She's fond of telling them how her son had made her proud and lives in a town called 'Mann-Home', as if it's a homestead in Kashmir just outside Srinagar." In fact there are many place-names in Kashmir ending in 'home'.

For ten years, Zulifkar had lived a parsimonious life in Baden-Württemberg and started to spend some money on himself only after setting up his own business. His cousin had advised him that he should buy trendy clothes and be well-groomed so that he looked like a successful businessman. In fact, Zulifkar worked in his pizzeria from mid-morning to late at night until he got married. He still worked longer hours than most of his staff. Jehangir advised him to cut his hours at his restaurant further in order to enjoy family life. I asked Zulifkar when was the last time he'd taken a break. "A few years ago," he replied, "when I got married in Kashmir."

The wealthy relatives who had shunned Zulifkar's family were now keen to attend his wedding and many of them hugged and kissed him on the forehead, as is customary in Kashmir, when they saw him dressed up as a groom. His family didn't borrow a Mercedes car, though, to drive him to his bride's home for the reception but had hired a tall horse for his ride. Zulifkar's father had his own horse when he was a child and used to ride up a hill in Srinagar to visit relatives living in the houses that were perched on the hill overlooking the town. Zulifkar was suspicious of his wealthier relatives. "I once visited one of them when I was a child. Because it was winter I wore a woollen cap. The girls at this relative's home mocked me – they said that I looked like a houseboy from some remote village in Kashmir. I feel more appreciative of my poor relations. They were kind to my family when we weren't doing so well."

The high point in Zulifkar's life journey from Srinagar to Baden-Württemberg was his wedding in Kashmir. Some of the elderly guests at the wedding reminisced about his great-grandmother's funeral when his grandfather had laid on a feast for hundreds of people who had come to his house to express their condolences. "It was half a century since my great-grandmother died but my older relatives still talked about her funeral. My grandfather had a special coffin made for his mother. As you know, people in Srinagar acquire a coffin from a local mosque to carry to the graveside, where the corpse is removed from the coffin and buried. The coffin itself is retained and re-used. My grandfather donated his specially made coffin to a mosque after his mother's burial because it spooked my family when he stored it at home."

The city of Mannheim suited Zulifkar better than Heidelberg. He had formed friendships in Mannheim with fellow-migrants, unlike his cousin whose friends and acquaintances in Leiman were exclusively German. The people who came to eat at his pizzeria were of various ethnicities but Zulifkar's friends were mostly Turkish. He went to a Turkish barbershop for his haircut, bought his groceries from a Turkish shop and liked to buy meat at a Turkish butcher.

A Turkish friend of mine in London called Ali had told me that the Turks who migrated to Germany to work in factories in the 1960s and 1970s were mostly from rural areas. Known as *Gastarbeiter* (guest workers), they expected to return home after a few years. Many decades had passed since then and most of them had become grandfathers but they still yearned to return to their villages in Turkey.

We passed a barbershop in Mannheim. The barber, who seemed to know Zulifkar, offered him an unhurried haircut and he took up the offer. There were two men working as barbers in the shop. The older one had grey hair and wore a white coat. Zulifkar told me that this man worked as a postman in the morning and a barber in the evening. He had saved enough from his two jobs to buy three or four houses in his village in Turkey. The shop was connected to a room at the back where the postman changed into his barber's white coat and hung up his postman's uniform. "He doesn't need a second job," Zulifkar said, "because the Deutsche Post pays him a fair wage, but he probably got into the habit of doing two jobs a long time ago and finds it difficult to change his routine."

Many Turkish people of his generation in Mannheim gathered in coffee-shops and restaurants and watched the news on Turkish TV channels. Some of them played cards throughout the day, and the expressions on their faces suggested a dreamy second life elsewhere.

Ali had told me that most of the *Gastarbeiter* had mistakenly believed, as did their German hosts, that they would return to their villages in Turkey after a few years. Ali was from Istanbul and very urbane compared to people who had left villages in Turkey and were lured by the prospect of finding work in Germany when there was a shortage of unskilled labour in the country. He told me that the stereotype of a Turkish immigrant as a provincial had persisted even though people from Istanbul are more sophisticated than many of the Germans living in Baden-Württemberg. I remember someone else once telling me how trains full of Turks seeking work arrived in Germany in those days. The joke going around was that Germany was nice except that there were too many Germans.

Zulifkar had invited a few Turkish friends to attend his wedding in Kashmir. He had informal business agreements with some of his friends whereas his cousin Jehangir liked to do everything by the book. It seemed to me that there was a kind of mutual understanding between Zulifkar and his Turkish business partners, facilitated by the fact that there are many common words in Turkish and the Kashmiri language. Those words in Kashmiri were borrowed from Urdu, which in turn borrowed them from Turkish. I was surprised to see Turkish written in Roman script when I visited Germany for the first time. The alphabet in both Kashmiri and Turkish has been changed – Sharada to Perso-Arabic in Kashmiri and the other way round in Turkish, from Perso-Arabic to Latin.

Zulifkar liked to use words that are common in both Turkish and Kashmiri while negotiating prices with his Turkish suppliers. His friendships with Turkish people had made it easier for him to advertise his restaurant by word of mouth to the sizable Turkish population in Mannheim. He had created a menu for the Turkish palate by serving a type of pizza known as *Lahmajoun*. He had learnt from his cousin to be experimental in creating a menu by blending various cuisines. Sometimes he failed and sometimes he succeeded in creating a topping that proved to be a hit with his customers. Although he didn't have any formal training in gastronomy his years of *in situ* experience served him well.

Jehangir emulated his German friends in doing things immaculately but Zulifkar's approach was more laissez-faire. However, both of them were successful in business and each of them wondered how the other had succeeded in tough places like Heidelberg and Mannheim since their approaches were diametrically opposed.

Zulifkar had a few tickets to see an ice hockey match at the SAP Arena located between Heidelberg and Mannheim. It was the home of his local team, The Mannheim Eagles. He invited me and his cousin to see the match. The seats were on the exclusive club level since Zulifkar was one of the sponsors of the venue and the name of his pizzeria was advertised at the entrance. "It cost me a lot of money to be a sponsor," he said. "Jehangir convinced me it was necessary to advertise there if I wanted to make it as a restaurateur in Mannheim. But I was reluctant to spend any more money on this way of advertising my restaurant. I'm looking for cheaper options."

I asked him about the name of the arena and he explained that SAP is a software company in Germany. He found the name of the ice hockey team amusing since the word for Eagle in Kashmiri has got negative connotations – it means a wicked person.

I had never seen a live ice hockey match before but Jehangir assured me it would be fun, and the spectators were very excited because their home team was playing that evening. Admittedly, I had seen ice hockey matches on television but to see one live was something else. The match turned out to be more like a musical extravaganza than a sports event because of the singing and dancing.

The club area was a meeting place for the business people of Mannheim and Heidelberg, and Jehangir chatted with them during the interval. He knew a few quite well and introduced his cousin to them. Jehangir was well-versed in the art of marketing new businesses and had even advised Zulifkar to make a provision for marketing expenditure in his budget before he opened a restaurant.

The town of Mannheim is laid out in quadrants with a baroque palace at its centre, part of which is occupied by the University. There is an ornate water tower known as Wasserturm in a horseshoe-shaped garden that protrudes from the circle and this tower can be seen from afar when approaching the city centre via the boulevard known as Augustaanlage. A replica of the first motorcar ever built by Karl Friedrich Benz in Mannheim is on display, mounted on a plinth. Augustaanlage is flanked by streets named after Nietzsche, Spinoza and Wagner. A nearby stadium has been named after Karl Benz. Zulifkar told me it was his ambition to open a pizzeria in Friedrichsplatz, which adjoins the Wasserturm.

Zulifkar was living in a flat above shops in one of the quadrants in central Mannheim. He found it convenient to live and work in the same area. I asked him if he planned to live in the same place indefinitely. "No," he said. "I'd like to move out of central Mannheim after a few years and also buy a plot of land in Kashmir." "Why would he buy land in Kashmir if he lives in Mannheim?" "Because nationalism is worryingly on the rise again in Germany and I want a place to go back to if I ever have to leave Mannheim. Some of the conversations I hear make me feel apprehensive about my future in this country. It was a different story when I came to Germany a decade ago." But now brutal events all over the world were changing the opinions and attitudes of people in Germany, as well as other countries, regarding multiculturalism.

He was more pragmatic than Jehangir, who idolized his adopted country. Zulifkar didn't take part in any activities outside his business and Jehangir thought his cousin was mad to be working such long hours. Jehangir told me it was very tempting as a business owner to do everything himself but he had learnt to delegate when he was an Area Manager of a fast food chain. Jehangir was concerned about his cousin's wellbeing and hoped that Zulifkar would change his lifestyle before it was too late. Zulifkar said that he had got into the habit of working long hours and would feel guilty if he only worked 40 odd hours a week like most people in Germany. Jehangir sympathised with him but considered it to be inefficient to work long hours every day. "Life is too short for such a grind. I enjoy leisure activities, like taking my mother-in-law's dog for a walk in my free time.

Some people referred to the Marktplatz in Mannheim as Little Istanbul, characterizing it as a ghetto, but Zulifkar liked it more than the Marktplatz in Heidelberg, which I had visited with his cousin. He felt it to be an essential part of the Turkish community in Mannheim. He had spent some time in Heidelberg but never felt as if he belonged there. I asked him what he thought of his cousin living in a small town in the state of Baden-Württemberg. Zulifkar said that he could never think of living in a place like Leimen. But Jehangir was married to a German woman and was therefore somewhat accepted by the Leiman community. Zulifkar was very grateful to his cousin for bringing him over to Germany and giving him the opportunity to work there. He didn't bemoan the wretchedness of that work.

"I could never have worked in a restaurant in Kashmir," he told me, "because it would have meant dishonouring my family. But I'm free to choose any kind of work in Germany. I want my wife to find a job when our toddler is ready to go to a nursery as it will give her a chance to get to know people living in Mannheim. She's learning German and has already made a few friends at the language school. I'm keen for her to learn German so she can help me with my business correspondence."

Zulifkar himself had never found the time to go to a language school. He had picked up conversational German at his places of work but he struggled to write a business letter in German. It was a disadvantage that Zulifkar shared with the first generation of Turks living in Mannheim yet it had turned into a bond of friendship and community. Since he had made several Turkish friends in Mannheim, I asked Zulifkar if he had ever been to Turkey. "Yes, I visited Istanbul once and enjoyed the trip. The city is gigantic. It makes me smile if someone compares the Marktplatz in Mannheim with such a big metropolis. I enjoyed smoking a Shisha (known locally as Nargile) in Beyoğlu and I've been to a hammam (Turkish baths) which I found very relaxing. It reminded me of my grandfather's hammam in Srinagar."

This in turn reminded me that I once bumped into Michael Palin in a shop in Hampstead. He had made a travel documentary, *Around the World in 80 Days*, for the BBC a few years earlier. I asked him if he had been to Kashmir. He hadn't, he said, but he knew that we had Turkish hammams in Srinagar.

It's a small world, I thought.

Berlin, Berlin

On my first visit to Germany in 1988 I took a train with my cousin from Hamburg to Berlin. The train passed through East Germany (GDR) to reach West Berlin and I had it very much in mind that I was travelling from a capitalist country into a communist one. I had often heard the terms 'First World' and 'Third World' but the link between these two worlds was somehow missing in my patchy adolescent knowledge. It wasn't until many years later, when I heard a lady in the foyer of a London hotel complaining about something and asking angrily if she was in "a Third World country", that I understood that such a classification is derogatory.

I accompanied my cousin on his trip to West Berlin to see one of his clients who owed him some money and hadn't paid him a penny for a long time. As we emerged from one of the local train stations in Berlin, I saw a badly damaged church spire along Kürfurstendamm avenue, surrounded by new buildings. It was easy to guess that the ruins of this church had been left there on purpose to remind onlookers of the horrors of war. It was my first sight of a World War II ruin in Germany.

A model of a perpetual motion machine was on display in one of the buildings near the church. As a student, I'd been fascinated by the idea of a machine that could run forever without an energy source. But it was a bizarre vantage point to see both the half-destroyed spire of a church that had been bombed in the War and the model of a machine that, unreliant on fossil fuel, might save our planet for generations to come.

We stayed in a small hotel in Berlin that was run, and perhaps owned as well, by two Afghan brothers. On our floor we met two women guests who couldn't open the door of their room and asked us for help. My cousin was able to open the door for them by what looked like sheer sleight of hand. He was tempted, I learned later, to have a peek into their bedroom but held to the principle that a gentleman does not enter the bedroom of a woman without her permission.

The next morning we left the hotel early to go and see the client. It was a surprise visit – my cousin hadn't informed his client beforehand about our visit to Berlin so he wouldn't dodge him. My cousin was lucky enough to find his elusive debtor sitting in his office that morning. However, the client claimed that he was unable to pay him anything. Since we had travelled to Berlin expressly to see him, my cousin lost his temper. The client walked out during the argument and we followed him onto the street. He wanted to get into his car but my cousin began shouting at him. An elderly woman walking down the road stopped to give my cousin a hug to calm him down. Perhaps the client felt a bit embarrassed because he agreed to negotiate new terms, on condition that he would talk only to me since I'd watched the drama without uttering a word. I felt flattered to be appointed an arbitrator at the youthful age of 19.

On our way back to the train station, I saw a crowd by the roadside watching a military parade by American troops stationed in Berlin. I had seen one or two American military aircraft on the ground at the Frankfurt airbase but certainly didn't expect to see American soldiers marching through the town half a century after the War ended.

Later, back home, when I met the tutor who was going to teach me German at Kashmir University, I mentioned that I had been to Berlin a few months earlier. He asked me if I had seen Checkpoint Charlie and a building that stood there known as the House of Tears – he liked to call it the House of Sorrows. 'Charlie' struck me then as an amusingly odd name for a barrier through which a visitor had to pass to get from one country to another.

The tutor, who taught us English at my Higher Secondary school in Srinagar told his class one day that if a wounded dog walking along a street was spotted by a German soldier, the dog would probably be shot dead for fear of spreading disease. But if a British soldier saw such a dog, he would (perhaps) take him to a vet for treatment. I was surprised that our teacher thought so highly of the British, who had colonised a quarter of the planet, including the Indian subcontinent, for over two hundred years.

I was in Hamburg in the summer of 1990 when Germany's reunification took place, and I occasionally heard the song, 'Berlin, Berlin, dein Herz kennt keine Mauern' – 'Berlin, your heart knows no walls'. The fall of the Berlin Wall in November 1989 had given people in Kashmir the false hope that very soon there would no longer be a 'Line of Control' (a de facto border) dividing Kashmir. They were very excited as they closely watched the uprisings in countries that belonged to the Eastern Bloc. However, there was despair a few months later when hundreds of people in towns and villages were killed by government forces.

My brief visit to Berlin before the Wall came down had the effect of urging me to visit the city again after three decades, in 2017.

In the meantime the city had again become the capital of a unified Germany, government offices and embassies having moved there from Bonn. Berlin began to attract people from all over Europe and beyond. It has become one of the most talked about cities in the world. An acquaintance who'd lived in Berlin for several years told me that a lot of people living in the city were actually very hard up and that I would see many rough sleepers in the town.

In fact I wanted to meet another acquaintance in Berlin who had moved there from London a couple of years ago.

I had booked accommodation in a hotel near Ostbahnhof in Berlin. The borough of Friedrichshain-Kreuzberg proved to be a good location to explore both East and West Berlin. A remaining part of the Berlin Wall serves as an outdoor art gallery because of its murals and it was within walking distance from the hotel, which turned out to be a pleasant surprise. I hadn't been near the Wall during my first visit to Berlin when it marked the border between East and West. It was hard not to be moved by standing in front of the wall that, like a carving knife, had divided Berlin into two halves. A section of the wall has a doorway cut through it that's fitted with a wrought iron door. I could see the river Spree flowing behind it and an industrial building on the other side of the river. Some people had put padlocks on the door as emblematic love-knots. A soldier in an Allied uniform stood behind a low table with many rubber stamps on it, stamping the passport of a tourist by way of a souvenir. But it must have been a real pain in Cold War days to go through checkpoints when travelling from one sector of Berlin to another.

I started my tour of Berlin on the east side of town. The bus drove along Karl-Marx-Allee, which is flanked by big buildings. Cars and houses in East Germany look a lot less austere, compared to those in the West, than they did during my earlier trip. Driving through such a monumental cityscape is like travelling back in time. Someone had hung a banner with a 'STOP WARS' slogan written on it from the window of a derelict building. The tall TV tower, with its golden dome, provides a flashy backdrop in an otherwise dull landscape. An old neon sign can be seen above the ground floor of a big building in this broad avenue of a former bookshop that, like the Allee, was named after Karl Marx.

The bookshop sign reminded me of the Soviet magazines published in India during my childhood. These magazines were produced on thick non-glossy paper with high-quality printing. A postman once left a copy of a Soviet magazine at my uncle's shop in Srinagar and when my uncle realised that I was keen to read it, he asked the postman to deliver a copy of it every month for me. The magazine published stories of people living happily in the Soviet Union and its satellite countries. It was published in various Indian languages, including Urdu. I was unaware at the time that this magazine was a mouthpiece of the Soviet Ministry of Information. The principal of our primary school occasionally pointed out to us at our morning assembly, by way of moral example, how workers in the Soviet Union worked for longer hours if they weren't happy with their working conditions rather than going on strike. Perhaps our principal also subscribed to 'Soviet Land' magazine.

Berlin, both East and West, appeared to be one vast building project. A new City Palace with an intricate brick façade is being built in the centre of the town. Visiting Berlin before the Wall came down was like entering a forbidden city. But the reunification of Germany has created many possibilities for Berlin's regeneration. New buildings are going up everywhere. A new airport is being built and one of the old airports has already been abandoned. A new main train station has been constructed like an iron and glass cathedral in the centre of the town. I saw the same sculpture of a giant steel horse outside the station as the one I had seen outside a glass building in Heidelberg. And many empty buildings have been turned into nightclubs or venues for various art projects. Berlin has attracted numerous artists and musicians since its reunification.

James is the name of my London acquaintance, the one who had moved to Berlin two years ago. James lives in Kreuzberg, like many artists and musicians who have moved to Berlin recently. I met him in Ostbahnhof for a coffee. He'd worked for a few years in London as a hotel barman by day and a DJ by night. James came from Rivers State in Nigeria and had lived in London for 15 years before moving to Berlin. He had travelled through Niger, Mali and Mauritania to reach Morocco and then crossed the sea by boat to get to Spain. He lived in Milan for a few months, selling trinkets to tourists in front of the Sforza Castle to earn enough money to reach Calais and then travelled across the English Channel hidden in a lorry. He told me that the UK was the country of his dreams and it was like a homecoming for him when he reached Dover. James was passionate about music and hoped that one day he would make his living just by being a DJ. The only European language he spoke was English.

James' father was a pastor in a small church in the Rivers State who wanted him to sing Gospel songs in his church and believed that James had gone astray because he was enthusiastic only about DJing. When I saw James for the first time he was working behind the bar in a London hotel, crushing ice in a bucket, mixing and shaking drinks and throwing glasses up in the air. Sometimes, late at night, I would see him carrying big speakers, amplifiers and a mixer on his way to a venue outside London where he played music. He usually changed from his barman's black uniform to a DJ's gear and wore a black baseball cap when he mixed tracks on his deck. He also wore over his T-shirt a gold chain with a pendant in the shape of Africa. He didn't earn much as a DJ, though, and relied on his job as a bartender to pay his bills.

James had lived in London for more than a decade without any validating documents before he married an Irishwoman and became eligible to apply for naturalisation as a British citizen. The family of his wife were very supportive and hired a lawyer for him to submit an application to the Home Office. They gave him five thousand pounds to pay his lawyer and various other fees involved. Although James loved his wife he still needed to prove that it wasn't a sham marriage in order to have it registered at his local town hall. James was grateful both to his wife for marrying him and to her parents for accepting him as their son-in-law.

He liked to roll tobacco into thin cigarettes and smoke a couple of them one after another. I had also seen him once or twice ducking behind his bar to swallow a shot of whiskey. He was so much into music that he spoke to his customers sitting at the bar about his night work while making cocktails for them. One day he was asked to make his own cocktail and give it a name. He named it 'R&B' and his fellow barmen seemed to like it.

London had proved to be hard work for James as it is for many of the town's inhabitants. The rent he paid for his small flat was very high. He had lived in a single room before he got married and even that was expensive. Some of the people who drank at the bar where he worked recommended that he move to Berlin since the city was less expensive than London and had a lot of nightclubs where he might stand a better chance of finding work as a DJ.

James told me that he was unable to leave the UK for 13 years before he was able to try his luck as a DJ in another European capital. By the time he arrived in Berlin in 2015 the city wasn't cheap any more. He had met various artists from all over the world in Berlin and found that most of them were broke. "To be an artist is to suffer", James said while reminiscing about his life in London and Berlin. But he didn't mind suffering for the sake of his passion in life and claimed that he preferred to live a frugal life and do his own thing. In Berlin he worked most days as a club doorman and as a DJ in various nightclubs once or twice a week. He was certainly DJing more often in Berlin that he had been in London.

James is tall and thin, unlike many nightclub doormen, who tend to be broad-shouldered and barrel-chested. But today there is a different breed of doorman in Berlin – there's even one who models for Hugo Boss.

I asked James in what ways his life in Berlin was different from the one he'd lived in London. "It's easier", he said, "to live a debauched life as a clubber in Berlin than in London.

But as a doorman I try to live a disciplined life except for smoking the odd joint for relaxation. I stay away from other drugs." He explained that as no photography is allowed, only clubbers in Berlin know what goes on inside the 'dark rooms' in many of the clubs. He himself worked as a doorman at one of the smaller clubs but he told me that some of the doormen at the better-known clubs had become celebrities.

James is father to a little girl who is three years old. His wife lives in London and works as a shop-assistant. His mother-in-law looks after his daughter when his wife is at work. "I'm not making enough money in Berlin," he said, "to afford to bring my family over to live with me. But I often travel to London to see them. My little girl is an angel who has saved my life. Without her I'd be living a debauched life like many of the musicians I've met in London and Berlin." When I asked James if the teachings of his father, who was a pastor, had any effect on him, he said that his father cared more about his congregation than his own children and hadn't taught him much. James loved his late mother but wished his father had played a bigger role in his upbringing.

James had grown up in Rivers State in Southern Nigeria. When I asked him about his town of birth, he said it was the state capital, Port Harcourt, but I heard it as 'Pathankot' – a town at the border of Jammu & Kashmir and Punjab. Port Harcourt had a vibrant nightlife scene and James went to what he called music joints in the evenings. "As a teenager I liked to listen to Fela Kuti's songs and fell in love with R&B. But it's difficult to be a full-time DJ if you only play R&B. As a DJ you have to play some hip-hop in nightclubs in London and Berlin even during the R&B nights they sometimes host."

Berlin is renowned for Techno nightclubs but computer-generated music doesn't interest James because he believes you have to be on cocaine to appreciate the tempo of this type of music. He pointed out for me that Berlin's most famous Techno nightclub was just a short distance from where we sat drinking coffee in the Ostbahnhof. "I know about Berlin's reputation as a paradise for hedonists and it's true that a lot of clubbers come from other European cities to visit Berlin's nightclubs. I sometimes spots clubbers from Britain waiting in line outside my club and I'll usually let them in before the others." As a doorman, James felt that he was working at the gates of Paradise by ushering clubbers into a nightclub late at night.

I wanted to ask James about his experience as a black man living in Berlin in the second decade of the 21st century. He burst into his usual unrestrained laughter. "It isn't the same as living in London," he said, "but I'm not bothered either by how some people see me through the prism of colour. The Kreuzberg where I live is very multicultural but you don't see as many black faces in Berlin as you do in London. He doesn't have the same sense of belonging that he feels in London. "It's rare in London that I'm made conscious of the colour of my skin but sometimes Berlin makes me aware of it. I get the same feeling when I travel to a small town in Ireland with my wife to see her relatives. But they all adore my little girl, who is prettier than either of us because of her mixed-race complexion."

James believes that most people forget the colour of your skin if you excel in your profession. The Techno clubs mostly attract a white clientele but James meets quite a few black men and women whenever he DJs in a club that hosts an R&B night. He certainly receives a lot more respect as a DJ than as a doorman.

I asked James if he had been back to Port Harcourt since he married. "I've travelled there just once," he said, "without my wife and daughter. I met my brothers and sisters again." Some of his old friends called him 'Oyinbo' – a person of European descent – since he had married a white woman, and they called his little girl an Oyinbo princess. His father, however, was not happy about his choice of profession.

How long was he going to stay in Berlin to make his name as a DJ? "Not long" was his quick reply. "I plan to live in Berlin for a few more months and then move back to London. I miss my wife and daughter and I want to live with them. It's tiring work as a doorman, standing in the same place for hours at a stretch."

Living in Berlin as he has for the past two years, James has got to know many people living there who have got heavily into debt. He himself had a huge debt for many years. He'd paid back most of it and knew it was a wretched way of living when half your salary goes into paying off debts. He had used a payday loan shop in London that charged an extortionate rate of interest – he would never set foot in that shop again. It was after the birth of his daughter that he resolved to pay off most of his debts.

I asked James to comment on what a friend in London had told me – that there are many rough sleepers in Berlin. "I've got sympathy with them," he said, " because I know what it's like to sleep on the street. I slept rough on the streets of Milan for some time. It's an experience I'll never forget. A lot of the rough sleepers in Berlin come from countries that once belonged to the Eastern bloc but are now part of the EU. To apply for housing benefit, you have to have an address, but these people don't have any money to rent a flat and provide an address and so they end up sleeping rough. I can never say no to a man or a woman who approaches me with outstretched hand if I have money in my pocket," he added ruefully.

The clubbers who fly to Berlin from other countries for a weekend have made the city a transient kind of place. James sometimes engages in chit-chat with the people queuing outside the nightclub but knows that he will never see them again. The bands that tour Berlin in their big coaches make it feel like a party town. The musicians stay in various hotels in the towns they play but their coaches are their real homes, truly mobile homes, since they spend so long on the road touring various cities in Europe. I saw a few such big coaches parked near the hotel where I stayed. There was a group of musicians checking into the hotel when I arrived and the lobby was full of metal cases on wheels in which they transport their musical instruments. James said that so many artists were moving from one city to another in search of a habitat that he felt as if the whole world was in a state of flux.

I wanted to know more about why James hadn't brought his wife and daughter to live with him in Berlin. "My wife relies on her parents," he said, "to look after our little girl while she works at a supermarket counter in London. Working in Berlin has given me an insight into the music industry," he added, "and it will help me when I move back to London." James gets by in Berlin just speaking English. He sometimes uses words that his wife, being Irish, is fond of using. For example, while chatting with me, he described something as 'grand'. I had worked with a German colleague from Berlin a few years ago who sounded like an American. A guest from Cheshire in the Midlands liked to call her "my American friend". She told me that there were more Americans living in Berlin than British. While travelling on trains in Berlin, I heard quite a few Americans talking to each other. At breakfast in the Berlin hotel restaurant, I overheard a candidate being interviewed for the position of a receptionist in the same hotel. The interview was being conducted in English.

When I asked James if he'd tried to learn German since he moved to Berlin, he said that there was no need since most Berliners spoke English as well. He had tried to improve his English in the fifteen years since he arrived in the British Isles. He spoke what is known as Pidgin English when he was in Port Harcourt. Only those Port Harcourtians who go in for higher education give much thought to speaking standard grammatical English. But James hadn't been to university. The lyrics of the songs by his favourite singer, Fela Kuti, were written in Pidgin English. It wasn't until James arrived in London that he realised that most native speakers didn't understand his broken English and so he tried learning the language anew. Just as Pidgin English became the lingua franca in many countries during the colonial era, Standard English has become the lingua franca of the music industry in our time.

When James left the Rivers State, his friends implored him not to forget them if he ever hit the big time. But a decade and a half had passed and he is nowhere near to realising his dream. When he goes back to London in a few months time he plans to try once again to get a break from working as a bartender or doorman to support himself and his family. He wants to produce his own music compilations. James works on his music when he isn't working as a doorman or a DJ in Berlin and gives away the CDs he's made to the clubbers he meets at the nightclub entrance. Living in Berlin on his own has helped James to compile an album of his own soundtracks that might help him to establish his reputation as a DJ. He unzipped his shoulder bag and gave me a CD of his album to keep.

It was already half past six when I finished chatting with James – time to go as I was due to take a train to Potsdamer Platz, a central location in Berlin. James directed me to the platform and suggested we meet again before I left Berlin.

I had seen a black and white poster at a train station the

night before that depicted a city devastated by war, with the caption 'Topographie des Terrors'. From a distance, I thought it was a picture of Aleppo but it turned out to be an advert for an exhibition about the Second World War and I decided on the spur of the moment to go and see it.

Direction signs for the exhibition hall were visible as soon as I came out of the train station at Potsdamer Platz. It had turned cloudy and there was drizzle in the air. I caught sight of the 'Topographie des Terrors' signboard. As I walked towards the gate, I saw a long line of English schoolchildren emerging from the exhibition hall. This hall is built on the site of the Third Reich's Gestapo and SS secret police headquarters. A group of German schoolchildren could be seen on a guided tour of the exhibition, listening attentively to a speaker who was giving them some facts and figures about the Second World War. I drifted into an area of the exhibition that displayed black and white photographs of the era preceding the war. They reminded me of the late-night black and white war documentaries shown by our public service broadcaster, Doordarshan, during my childhood in Srinagar. These photos, showing Nazis in their uniforms, looked very sinister. There was an eerie silence in the hall, as if the people looking at these pictures were reflecting on how the Weimar Republic, a democratically elected government, could have brought forth such a murderous regime. The silence was broken by the sound of the schoolchildren applauding the exhibition guide.

I saw an old couple gazing at a photograph with tears

in their eyes. It was a haunting image, showing a frail-looking man being forced into a wagon constructed in the shape of a crocodile's open jaws, with the words 'Der Judenfresser' written on it in big letters. I remembered my tutor telling me that the meaning of 'fresser' is devourer. I wondered whether the couple looking at the picture were Jewish. Whether or not, it was a moving sight.

A clock struck eight, the lights in the exhibition hall went off suddenly, and an announcement was made that everyone should leave as the exhibition was closed. I felt disconcerted at having seen only a part of the exhibition and resolved to return to this unsettling place if I ever visited Berlin again.

A Bend in the River Spree

On my third day in the capital city, I wanted to explore what Berliners like to call *Mitte*. There was indeed a time when Mitte was the centre of the town but then it was merged with other districts to form a borough. It includes a big English country-style park called Tiergarten. I hadn't expected to see an English garden in the heart of a German city. At the edge of this park stands the Reichstag, which has the English architect Norman Foster's glass dome built above it. Because English is widely spoken in Berlin, you could be forgiven for thinking that the capital of Germany is still under occupation.

Many new embassies have been built around the Tiergarten since the capital was reassigned from Bonn. As the bus I was travelling in drove past the Mexican embassy, its inclined pillars in the façade created an optical illusion of movement. It was like walking past some cleverly built bookcases in the foyer of The British Library that seem to rotate when you look at them while walking through the hall. A newly built Indian embassy features an exterior of red stones shipped from Rajasthan. The Russian embassy in Berlin is palatial since it was built during the days of GDR. The only building in front of the Reichstag to survive the devastation of World War II displays a red flag with a white cross in the middle and houses the Swiss embassy, the very embassy in which Swiss diplomats entertained Nazi officials during the Third Reich. This embassy is surrounded by a barren, treeless park delineated by a bend in the River Spree.

The German embassy in Delhi is housed in a modern building in a diplomatic enclave but its cultural centre occupies a colonial-style house in Kasturba Gandhi Marg near Connaught Circus. I lived in Delhi for a few months in the early 1990s and regularly visited the reading room of the Goethe-Institut, as it is known, to escape the heat, which greatly helped make my stay bearable during the summer months. The venue is known as Max Mueller Bhavan, named after a German Indologist who translated the Upanishads into English. I have always marvelled at his accomplishment as he had never been to India..

The Max Mueller Bhavan reading room was less crowded than the nearby British Council and the American Centre in Delhi but I was happy to find a few eccentrics using it. Among the regulars was a lady whom I had mistaken for a serious scholar until I noticed that she was not actually reading but only staring at the pages of upheld cookery books. A long-haired man always sat at the top end of the large oval table there. When I asked him once for help in translating a German text into English he told me that he didn't speak a word of German. A German woman married to a native of Delhi came to use the reading room wearing traditional Indian clothes. A silver-bearded man habitually talked to himself in the reading room. I once fell into conversation with him at the tea-stall outside. He told me that his parents came from Kashmir. His father, who had worked for the Ministry of External Affairs, had lived in many countries across the globe. He claimed that he was born in Tokyo. When I asked him about his line of work he said that he was going to get a 'top job' soon and I realized that he was probably daydreaming about some diplomatic post while sitting in the Goethe-Institut. His parents were Kashmiri Pandits but he hadn't been to Kashmir for many years. I felt a kind of kinship with him since we hailed from the same town and both sought respite from Delhi's heat within the thick walls of the Max Mueller Bhavan room.

I saw the new American embassy in Berlin, the design of which has caused consternation among Berliners because security needs have rendered its façade blankly unimaginative, like the exterior of a prison block. It looks utterly nondescript compared to the stylish Mexican embassy building. I also saw a new block of identical buildings that will be used as the headquarters of the German secret service. I recalled my friend Jehangir telling me that he had once met a foreign politician in Heidelberg and often glanced over his shoulder to see if the man was being followed by a secret service agent. I'd found this amusing at the time and thought Jehangir was unduly alarmed. Probably not so, it now occurred to me, when I saw the size of the headquarters of the German secret service – BND or *Bundesnachrichtendienst*. Since 'Nachrichten' means 'news', it's perhaps used as a euphemism for intelligence in today's Germany.

I noticed a lot more Afghan men in Berlin this time around and most of them were young. Many of these young men carried satchels and put gel on their hair like other teenagers in Berlin to make it look spiky. They had recently arrived in Germany and travelled on trains and buses in twos and threes. I heard a couple of them chatting to their friends in Farsi.

A group of Afghan and Syrian teenagers were being guided by a German tutor on a bus journey through the town. She was in her twenties and of cheerful disposition, readily engaging her students, who spoke halting German, in conversation. As the bus passed a building with a high perimeter wall and concertina razor wire above it, the tutor pointed towards the building, informing her group that it was a 'gefängnis', which I recalled meant 'prison' in English. The teenagers looked alarmed. It was perhaps a subtle warning for them to stay on the right side of the law lest they end up in clink. In fact, such teenagers have escaped brutal wars in their own countries and Germany has offered them the chance of an unshackled life.

James the DJ had told me he had a friend in Berlin from Lagos in Nigeria. I wanted to meet her to learn more about the life of Africans living in the city. Her name is Bola, a common Yaruba name for both women and men in Nigeria.

Like James, she is a musician but has lived in Berlin longer than him and has had more luck as an artist. She attained a degree in music from a university in America and her father is a senator in Abuja.

James had arranged for us to meet in a lofty-sounding coffee-shop near Alexanderplatz. Discovering coffee-shop chains in Berlin named 'Balzac' and 'Einstein' persuaded me that the city is indeed a distinguished place.

Bola had moved to Berlin from Boston because she wanted to live in Europe. But her father didn't approve of her carefree lifestyle and wanted her to get married and settle down. She had always been a rebel in her family, she told me. Her brothers and sisters were all married. She was in her early thirties and certainly in no rush to settle down. "It's the corruption in Nigeria," she said, "that made me rebel when I was in my mid-teens." Her father had sent her to America to study music. "My family was very religious. My father was sent to prison for speaking out truthfully when General Sani Abacha was in power." Abacha had deposited millions of dollars into his bank accounts in Switzerland which the Swiss government has recently agreed to return to Nigeria.

Bola considered her years at an American university very formative. Her parents visited her often when she was in Boston but had been to Berlin only once to see their daughter. Her parents weren't fond of Germany. I asked Bola about her mother. She told me that her mother didn't work but was involved in various charity projects.

There are more Ghanaians than Nigerians living in Berlin. In fact, Bola's boyfriend comes from Ghana. The Nigerians usually didn't get along well with their Ghanaian neighbours, and so Bola's parents didn't approve of her boyfriend, advising her that there were many well-to-do Nigerian men who would be happy to marry her.

Bola, who wore her hair short and sported large earrings, was proud of her African heritage. She was a vocalist and sang at different venues in Berlin. I asked her which Nigerian musicians she liked the most. "I have huge respect for Sade", she replied. "She can still fill an arena like SAP in Mannheim in no time. She's accomplished a lot as a musician. But she still prefers to live a quiet life in the Cotswolds in England."

I asked Bola, an R&B and Soul singer, if she had ever played at a venue in Nigeria. "Only once," she said, "at a fundraising event in Lagos." She was propositioned by a lot of men after the event, many of whom were married. Was Bola's boyfriend also a singer? "No, he's a doorman," said Bola, bursting into spontaneous laughter.

Curious to learn about her experience as an African in Berlin and Boston, I asked Bola how she felt about living in these two very different cities. She said that America was built on slavery and Britain had colonised her country for a long time. "Germany has experienced a very dark period in its history" she said, "but living in Berlin for me is no different from living in Boston. I saw race riots in many American cities when I studied at university there." Bola told me that she had felt offended only once while living in Berlin, when someone had inserted an 'E' before her name on a poster, turning it into 'Ebola' – this was during the outbreak of the disease in Africa. However, Bola had frequently felt insulted at Boston University where her fellow students often made sarcastic remarks about both Nigeria and Africa in general.

Bola had a privileged upbringing in Lagos. Her mother employed several nannies to look after her children while she was busy with her voluntary work. Though Bola was in her thirties, her parents still helped her with any major expenses. Bola cherished the idea of financial independence and as an upstart musician had to work very hard for every penny she earned. "I didn't need to lift a finger when I lived in Lagos", she said "but I couldn't bear the thought of living at home as an obedient daughter". Respect for elders was paramount for Nigerian children living at home. Most of her Nigerian friends kept their heads down and didn't speak much in front of their parents.

Bola's boyfriend and James were friends and sometimes manned the door of a nightclub together. When I mentioned that she looked very youthful with her cropped hair and big costume jewellery, she giggled and said "If I ever visit my ancestral village in Western Nigeria again, my relatives will say that I'm well past my sell-by date. But I like to live a nomadic life and I don't intend to raise a family any time soon. Berlin is actually only the second city I've lived in after Boston and I want to explore other European capitals like

London, Paris and Vienna."

I asked Bola when was the last time she had been to Lagos. "It was a year ago. As it happened, one of my friends from Berlin called Brigitte had moved to Lagos a year and a half earlier. She'd been keen on working in Africa for some time and my mother had arranged a job for her. When I met Brigitte in Lagos, she seemed to be happy living there and had found a boyfriend. They plan to marry eventually."

Having heard mention of an African Quarter in Berlin I wanted to learn more about this neighbourhood. I had once mistaken the Latin Quarter in Paris for a South American area whereas it turned out to be known for its educational institutions. Bola told me that the African Quarter in Berlin was in the neighbourhood of Wedding (the name amused me), which by coincidence I'd passed through by bus only the evening before. "Actually, I don't know the African Quarter that well. But my boyfriend has a few friends from Ghana living there and he sometimes goes to see them there."

Ten years ago, in London, I had met a journalist from a German magazine who had come to the UK to find out why so many people from outside the EU wanted to live and work in London rather than one of the big German cities. I had met her on the 6th of July – the day before bombs exploded in the London Underground. Two days later she was joined by colleagues who came to report on this tragic event. Her report had become a long feature article but its theme remained the same. Perceptions about Germany have changed since 2007 and many people now prefer to live in a German city rather than one in Britain. I mentioned to Bola that, according to some people, Germany let in a million men, women and children during the last two years because it wanted to redeem itself for past sins. "I think that's a cynical thing to say," Bola responded. "Most of these refugees have escaped brutal wars in countries like Syria, Iraq and Afghanistan. It should be an obligation for any country to give refuge to people who have escaped conflicts like those. I've also heard some people saying that Germany has an ageing population and needs displaced people to care for the elderly and work in factories, but I disagree with them." Bola knew about the dark period in Germany's history when Berlin had been the capital of the Third Reich. But she was equally aware of atrocities committed during the Biafran War in her own country before she was born. Her parents had many Igbo friends who were killed during that war.

Bola's father was a Christian and her mother a Muslim. I asked Bola about her own faith and she replied that she was more inclined towards the teachings of Rastafarianism than the religions of her parents. "Some of my close relatives are Christians and some of them are Muslims", she said. "Nigeria is one of the very few countries in the world where you can find one brother who's a Christian and the other is a Muslim. The country has an equal population of Muslims and Christians and some people who were born into one faith have converted to the other as adults."

The naming of some of the streets in Berlin's African Quarter after German colonists is controversial. This neighbourhood was planned a century ago. "The Germans at least own up to their role in the colonisation of Africa," Bola informed me, "but you can still find some apologists for imperialism in Britain and France. Nazis didn't only discriminate against the Blacks – they were against every race that they deemed inferior to their own Aryan race." One of her friends in Lagos was of mixed German and Nigerian heritage. Bola could see how mixed race must have represented quite a problem for the Nazis and how a black athlete like Jesse Owens challenged their notion of racial superiority by winning four gold medals in the Berlin Olympics of 1936.

I asked Bola if she had found a place among fellow musicians and artists in Berlin. "All of my credit cards are maxed out", said Bola, "but I'm not alone in this – there are a lot of people like me in Berlin. Everyone is broke, or in persistent debt, which makes me feel at home." She had undergone minor surgery a few months ago and taken some time off. Her parents had come to see her when she was in hospital and given her some money so she could convalesce without financial worries. They had stayed in the Adlon – a legendary luxury hotel near the Brandenburg gate. But Bola said that she didn't like to be waited on hand and foot and preferred to stay in a budget hotel whenever she travelled elsewhere in Germany. Bola's desire for independence persists.

While walking through the lobby of a high-rise hotel in Alexanderplatz to get to the other side of the building, I noticed a reproduction of one of Hieronymus Bosch's paintings on a brochure in a rack. Evidently there was an exhibition of his work in town so I picked up a copy of the brochure to find out where it could be seen. In fact, it wasn't that far from my hotel so I decided to go there at once. I crossed the new City Palace, which is currently under construction, and asked a lady for directions. She pointed to a distant building with a banner hanging on its façade. The actual venue of the exhibition was an old mint hidden behind this building and it took me a while to find its entrance. A great thing about Berlin is the way it makes use of old empty buildings for art projects.

The multimedia exhibition celebrated the 500th anniversary of Hieronymus Bosch's death. I have always been fascinated by this Dutch painter's macabre works. I entered a dimly lit room that included a ticket counter and a pop-up bar. The first canto of Dante's *Inferno* was written on a black wall in white ink with a resonance that then, as now, rang true for me.

'Midway upon the journey of our life
I found myself within a forest dark,
For the straightforward pathway had been lost.'

Music lured me into the exhibition mounted in an adjacent room. Small sections of *The Garden of Earthly Delights* were projected on the room's large walls. Every action in Bosch's painting was captured as if by a slow-motion camera. I took a seat on a bench facing one of the walls and watched the fantastical creatures in Bosch's work come to life. Images of Heaven were projected onto one wall and of Hell on the other.

There were a few beanbags on the floor and I was tempted to lie back in one of them. It was a different experience. The continuously changing images accompanied by an elegiac soundtrack created a kind of psychedelic pandemonium. The image of a small fish eaten by a big fish that in turn is being eaten by some other monstrous creature is powerfully allegorical and I got drawn in to the multiplicity of images in Bosch's painting as I lay transfixed on the floor.

Since I had come across the brochure of the exhibition by chance, this multimedia show of Hieronymus Bosch's work was an unexpected treat for me in Berlin. It was an impressive example of the media, music and tech start-up projects that are attracting many people to Berlin today.

Continuing my tour of Berlin's Mitte district, I saw an enormous concrete cube which, built as an air-raid shelter in 1943, was simply known as The Bunker. The word 'bunker' entered our Kashmiri lexicon in 1989 when such shelters were built at many crossroads in Srinagar, but they were ramshackle structures made of sandbags with corrugated iron sheets for roofs. I was surprised to see that The Bunker in Berlin has many architectural features and the building has been used as a nightclub and an art gallery. Some of the bunkers in Srinagar have been removed after a quarter of a century and many others are still occupied by paramilitary troops. The Führerbunker in Berlin, which was designed by Albert Speer, has been demolished and turned into a car park. Churchill's wartime bunker in Westminster – called the 'War Rooms' to make it sound grand – still survives, though I have yet to pay it a visit.

When gunfights between soldiers and militants became a common occurrence in Srinagar, I heard someone using the verb 'to open' to denote the firing of a gun – an unusual usage in the Kashmiri language, so I knew he was translating an English news report literally into Kashmiri. When I was growing up in Srinagar the news reports on Radio Kashmir often claimed that police had found guns and magazines in a hiding place and I wondered what popular periodicals had to do with weaponry. It was only many years later, when I saw pictures of guns and magazines on state television, that I understood that the word 'magazine' has more than one meaning.

One day at my secondary school, a new history teacher introduced himself to our class. Though he had a full head of white hair he seemed more energetic than his years. The teacher began to tell us stories of World War II, although it was beyond the scope of our textbooks. We were agape listening to his stories of Kamikaze pilots and their derring-do. He got the whole class excited by his anecdotes and we would eagerly await the next day's lesson to hear more of them. The real horrors of World War II dawned upon me years later when I learnt that more than 50 million people were killed in that relatively short span of time in what we regarded as civilized countries.

Travelling around Berlin, I found that one of the roads was called Colditzstrasse, which brought to mind the stories of our history teacher about a POW camp at Colditz. Towns with such names as Colditz and Weimar had become mythical places for me after hearing about them in my childhood.

It was a bright day and I decided to see Berlin on board a boat sailing up and down the River Spree. I had heard about Berlin being a glacial valley but the landscape appeared very flat compared to the Vale of Kashmir and I wasn't sure how Berlin could qualify as a valley since I hadn't seen any peaks and troughs in the town. The only mountain I'd heard of in Berlin was The Devil's Mountain and it turned out to be a man-made hill. As for the Spree, I had seen a black and white photograph of the frozen river under a bridge and a man in a long coat swept by wind walking on one of its banks. It looked a most inhospitable place to be in winter.

In the spring sunshine, however, the river looked cheerfully bright. The boat travelled first in the direction of the so-called 'Museum Island' (there are four or five museums there) and then turned to sail back to its starting point. The golden dome of a synagogue sparkled in the sun. It was a new synagogue built on the site of an old one. Berlin is attracting Jewish people again, many of them musicians and artists. I remembered once asking an acquaintance who worked in a clothing shop in Regent Street about his employer. He told me the owner of the shop was *Jewish* and *German*, putting emphasis on both words as if it was a double affliction.

There was something gleaming at a distance and the captain of the boat announced on the loudspeaker that it was a victory column from the time of the Prussian Empire and had been moved from its original location by the Nazis during the war.

While waiting at a bus stop, I noticed an advert for a budget airline stating 'Inländer Raus', the opposite of 'Ausländer Raus' – the words I had heard in a park in Leiman. Perhaps Berliners' reputation for having a dark sense of humour is justified.

For many years, I thought of Berlin principally as the city where Vladimir Nabokov lived before emigrating to America in 1937 with his son, Dmitri, and his wife, Vera, who was Jewish. Nabokov worked as a language tutor in Berlin but didn't feel at home in the city due to the disappointments of émigré life. I was once asked by a friend what was my favourite German word was and I spontaneously replied that it was *unheimlichkeit* which for me meant not being at home. However, when I asked a German colleague its precise meaning, she found it difficult to translate into English.

The Hotel am Steinplatz, where Nabokov stayed regularly, has opened again as a hotel after eight decades. When I first decided to travel to Berlin, I very much fancied staying there but realized it was too opulent for me. Nabokov's family had fled Russia after the Bolshevik revolution and his father was murdered in Berlin. Nabokov held a Nansen (stateless person's) passport for many years. In his autobiography, *Speak, Memory*, he describes the Nansen passport as 'a very inferior document of a sickly green hue. Its holder was little better than a criminal on parole and had to go through most hideous ordeals every time he wished to travel from one country to another, and the smaller the countries the worse the fuss they made.' One day I met a guest at our hotel whose surname was Nabokov and I asked her jokingly if she was related to the famous writer. She said yes very shyly, which made me feel great respect for her.

I wanted to travel outside Berlin for half a day and spotted Potsdam on a map at the end of a train line. When growing up in Kashmir I had heard the name Potsdam many times in connection with the famous post-war conference but hadn't realized until now that it was a small town just outside Berlin.

The station at the end of the line looked newly built. I asked a lady at the information counter how to get to the Sanssouci summer palace. She wrote a bus number on a piece of paper and thrust it into my hand, then brusquely showed me the door.

I wasn't sure where to get off the bus to reach the palace and asked a fellow passenger to let me know where I should alight. The bus drove through the town and then through green fields before the lady told me to get off at the next stop.

This turned out to be a stop too early. The gravel road, flanked by a row of tall trees, resembled an impressionist painting. The palace was located at the far end of a huge park. It was the beginning of spring and a few bright blue grape hyacinths could be seen in the green grass. The park appeared to be quite empty except for a solitary cyclist with a baby trailer attached to her bike riding through it. She told me that the nearest bus stop was on the other side of the palace. I inwardly groaned. However, it was a nice day and I enjoyed the long walk.

The Sanssouci palace is built on the scale of Versailles but the Potsdam Conference had taken place at another venue in the town. One of the rooms in the palace displays on its walls only black and white photographs of the paintings that disappeared during the war. The Russian troops had used the palace as shelter after the fall of Berlin. The Third Reich had tried to fulfil the dream of the Prussian Emperor by pushing eastwards to encompass more land and it had proved to be its nemesis.

On my return to Mitte, I drifted into Bebelplatz where Nazis had burnt books in the square. It was unsettling to recall that cheering crowds gathered at such book-burning rituals. Our history teacher, who'd told us so many stories of heroism during World War II, never delved into such details. It was brave of Foyles, the London booksellers, to offer to buy all the books that the Nazis were consigning to the flames, especially taking into account how meagre were the chances of making a profit from re-selling books printed in German. I recalled the case of Rose Ausländer – herself an exile – whose first collection of poems was pulped by the Nazis. It took her two decades to publish a second book.

As I travelled back to London, I remembered having seen Albert Speer's model of the city of Berlin that the Nazis planned to build anew. It evoked a phantasmagoria of horror in my mind – rather like one of Hieronymous Bosch's paintings. Berlin is also the city in which Fritz Lang's futuristic dystopian film, *Metropolis*, is set. The name of this remarkable city always reminds me of the liberal philosopher, Isaiah Berlin. But it is that dark period when Berlin was the capital of the Third Reich which overshadows everything else in its twentieth century history. In the new millennium, though, Berlin has again become a beacon of liberalism in the world. Perhaps that won't be for much longer because, as I write, nationalism is gaining a foothold once more.

❧

An English Garden in Munich

I travelled to Munich by train from Hamburg in 1990 to meet a client of my uncle. It was a long train ride through a green landscape with tall factory chimneys rising here and there, billowing smoke at the horizon. I had planned to be in Munich well before the time of my meeting but the train got delayed and I found myself running a few minutes late for my appointment. I rushed to the office of the person I was going to meet and apologized for being late before greeting him. He smiled and said that he knew that Asians are usually late for meetings, a reply that embarrassed me. Having lived in Germany for a few months, I knew about the German obsession with timekeeping but wasn't expecting such a response to being only 10 minutes late.

I caught the train back to Hamburg soon after my meeting and therefore didn't get to see Munich until I went there again in 2017 to meet an acquaintance called Derek and to explore this, the third biggest city in Germany. Derek had worked as a security guard in London for 12 years before moving to Munich. He hailed from Krakow but left Poland during the Cold War in the early 1980s, seeking refuge in

West Germany, and then lived in many countries in Europe and North America. He was planning to retire early in a year or two and move back to Krakow, the town of his birth.

I had got to know Derek when he worked as a security guard at a venue in London. Having worked as a labourer on construction sites for many years, he considered that working as a security guard was easy in comparison. He mostly worked at functions like Jewish weddings and Bar Mitzvahs in various hotels in London and usually talked to elderly people attending these functions in Polish. Derek had been to Jerusalem on a pilgrimage a few years earlier. And he was familiar with the rituals and practices of many religions, having worked with many people of different faiths.

As the aircraft taxied toward the terminal after landing, it passed two big military charcoal-grey transport planes that had small German flags painted on their tails and iron crosses on their fuselages. Before the plane landed I had looked out of the window in hope of seeing the Bavarian Alps but it was a completely flat landscape. However, it was colourful, like a patchwork quilt made of dark and light green hues and the brown of the newly sown fields.

I had arranged to meet Derek near the centre of town but he rang and told me to avoid Marienplatz as the Bayern Munich football team was celebrating their championship title in the square and he suggested that we meet instead near the main train station. I was staying at a hotel near the airport and took a train from there to reach the station. There were groups of men draped in FC Bayern München flags on their way to Marienplatz. Some of them were already drunk. A man walking in the opposite direction was unthinkingly wearing an England cap with a St. George's cross, which so infuriated the Bayern Munich fans that one of them snatched the cap and tossed it to the ground. The man picked up his cap and put it back on, murmuring a few swearwords in English. This enraged the Bayern Munich fan even more and he tried to snatch it again but was restrained by others as they let the England supporter go.

There are so many cafés and restaurants in the subterranean hallways that connect the local station with the main station in Munich that I wondered if anyone in the town ever ate at home. Derek was waiting for me in one of the coffee-shops. He is a Bayern Munich supporter and was jubilant that they had won the championship again. When he lived in London Derek had been a supporter of Millwall FC. I was surprised by his choice of this team when he first told me about it. Derek told me that since he lived in South East London Millwall was his local team and so he supported it from the day he moved into the district.

It was like being in a time-loop for Derek to be back in Germany. I asked him about his next destination and he said it was going to be the town of his birth, Krakow. "I'm planning to go to live there in a couple of years," he said. He had been saving for a long time for his early retirement. "I've saved money in each country I've worked in and so I hold bank accounts in many different currencies. I want to consolidate all my savings into a single account before moving back to Poland. I've got enough savings to see me through my retirement. I inherited a house in Krakow from my father – he passed away a year ago." When Derek got divorced from his wife, the court ruled that he pay for the maintenance of his daughter until she became an adult so he had been paying a few hundred pounds each month for the last ten years. This was going to finish soon as his daughter was about to come of age. I asked him the reason for the divorce. He sighed and shook his head. "It's my wife's parents who are to blame. They made it impossible for me and my wife to live together."

Derek had worked on construction sites in Chicago and as a house painter in Sweden and Finland before taking a job as a security guard in London. He works as a security guard in Munich as well. He suffered from backache when he worked as a labourer and decorator and found the security job far easier. He had moved to London before Poland joined the EU in 2004 when there were not many Polish people working in the UK. "But then I saw coaches arriving at Victoria station from Poland full of people looking for work. They were mostly young men and women half my age. I met many of the new arrivals at various places and tried to speak to them in Polish but when some of them answered in English I thought perhaps the time had come for me to travel in the opposite direction – from London to Krakow.

The exchange rate between the zloty and the British

pound was high when Poland joined the EU but it gradually began to sink until the new generation in Poland didn't see much attraction in moving to London. "I very much regret saving my money in London in British pounds and won't get as much money in zlotys when I move back to Poland. But I'm going to be okay financially because the utility bills for the house I've inherited in Krakow are very low." Derek loved to travel and thought it absurd to pay for two accommodations – the flat he rented in London and whichever one he rented during his holidays abroad. Sometimes he gave up his accommodation in London and left his belongings with friends before travelling for a few weeks but it was usually quite a rigmarole to hunt for a studio flat in London. Since he worked for an agency on a self-employed basis, his job as a security guard offered him the flexibility to work for a few months without taking a day off and then go on holiday for a few weeks.

The agency sent him to various locations in London. He had worked in the famous auction house, Christie's, where he sometimes carried a precious artwork for a seller and received a hefty tip. He had also worked for a number of businesses from art galleries to nightclubs in the town. "I was doing odd jobs after I arrived in London until one day someone told me I should do a security training course and apply for a license from the Home Office." Whenever I saw Derek at his place of work, he wore a lanyard with a badge issued by the Security Industry Authority attached to it, but most of the time he kept it in his shirt pocket. Although it cost him a few hundred pounds to renew his badge every three years, he was thankful for the Home Office accreditation as it had saved him from having to take casual jobs in London. Derek had paid the renewal fee for his security badge before moving to Munich. This had made it easier for him to find a job as a security guard there.

Derek is a big man, well suited to a job as a security guard. It is a 9 – 5 occupation. He'd worked for 12 hours a day in London and, like James, had found it tiring to stand for so many hours by the door in one place. Sometimes he rushed from one location to another to fulfil jobs on separate sites, working continuously for 24 hours. However, he was taking it easy now in Munich, winding down before his retirement.

After getting a divorce from his wife, Derek never wanted to marry again. He had found a girlfriend, though, in each city he ever lived and worked in but none of these relationships were of a profound kind. He'd had a Lithuanian girlfriend in London. When I asked him if he was still in a relationship with her, Derek said that it had ended the day he moved to Munich. He didn't expect her to follow him, though, any more than he expected his previous girlfriend in Sweden to follow him to London. His bitter divorce had made him emotionally a tough person because the financial implications of the divorce had lasted most of his working life. He always kept his finances separate from his girlfriend's and thought it necessary that she pay her own bills.

Derek had risked everything when, as a young man, he left Poland to live in Germany but now he was looking forward to moving back to Krakow. He told me how grim everything was in Poland and other Soviet satellite states in the pre-Glasnost period. "Krakow is attracting a large number of international tourists these days so I feel optimistic about renting out my flat in Krakow on a short let whenever I decide to travel for a few weeks. I plan to spend some money on doing it up. I've paid enough money to my landlords in the last 35 years and I'm glad that no landlord will extract rent from me anymore. My place in Munich isn't as expensive as my studio flat in London but it's still dear. I certainly couldn't afford to rent a flat in London without my girlfriend paying half the rent."

Krakow isn't that far from the Czech Republic and Slovakia and Derek plans to visit both of these countries regularly after moving back to his home-town. One of his previous girlfriends was from the Czech Republic and he speaks a bit of Czech. When he was based in London he explored Britain from John o' Groats to Land's End and also visited Northern Ireland. He loves to travel and always keeps a backpack ready at his home.

Derek has made many friends in various countries. He'd particularly warmed to Jewish people when he met them at their social events in London. "Krakow had a sizable Jewish population before the War," he told me. "But sadly my home-town became the capital of Germany's occupying General Government during the Nazi era and they confined all the Jews living in the city to a ghetto. I usually kept a list of names of the people attending a wedding or a Bar Mitzvah on a clipboard. I knew from the surnames which ones are of Polish ancestry and I usually greet them with more warmth and fervour."

While living in the UK, Derek had got to know many Arabs as well and made a few friends among them. When he visited Jerusalem to take part in a pilgrimage, he was asked at the airport in Tel Aviv if he had any Arab friends and whether he had been to an Arab country. "I was taken aback by such a question as I'd planned to travel to Jordan after visiting Jerusalem. Would I be refused entry to Israel when I told them that? I felt very uncertain."

I asked Derek about his decision to return to the town of his birth after living in many cities around the world. Quoting Voltaire, he replied that like Candide it was time for him to tend his own garden. Derek was born in the 1960s and grew up during the Communist era. His father had witnessed the devastation of World War II at firsthand, including the widespread looting by the Red Army. Although Derek loathes authoritarian communist regimes he is no fan of the capitalist order, having seen many inequalities in America and Western Europe. He still suffers pain in his spine from his hard graft in Chicago. He is eagerly waiting to return to the town of his childhood and live a more comfortable life.

Derek likes parks and gardens and wanted to show me the English Garden in Munich. He described it as a jewel in the crown of the city, one of the largest urban parks in the world. When Derek lived in London he often strolled through Hyde Park and St James Park on a sunny day if he wasn't working. The summer months are a near-festive time when both Londoners and tourists are drawn to Hyde Park and Kensington Gardens. The roller-skaters and skateboarders put on an impressive show and it's fun to watch their spectacular feats as one stands by the roadside along the Serpentine. Derek told me that there is a Holocaust Memorial Garden in Hyde Park; sometimes he would sit there halfway through his brisk walk and then carry on along the boating lake past a restaurant called The Magazine, designed by Zaha Hadid. I was intrigued by its name and, given my former misapprehension, should not have been surprised when I learnt that it used to be an old armoury.

Derek would cross Carriage Drive to reach the Italian Gardens before catching a train to work from Queensway. There are English-style gardens all over the world but Italian gardens are flourishing across England and you sometimes see them in the courtyards of gated houses in London. A German hotel guest who had been to Kashmir once told me that he was invited by someone in Srinagar to his home on the shore of Lake Nagin and found that his host's house was surrounded by an English garden.

Knowing that I commute to work in London on a bike, Derek suggested that I do a guided bike tour of Munich and that he would join me on the ride. I readily agreed.

When I met Derek for the first time in London, I thought he resembled a Munich police detective in the TV series *Derrick* who was over six feet tall. Derek is actually taller than the actor who played the detective in the series. I had never seen Derek riding a bike. He went to a shop in London called High & Mighty to buy his clothes and shoes and confided in me one day that he doesn't fit a Queen-size double bed when he stays in a hotel.

I certainly felt tempted in Berlin to jump on a bike after seeing so many designated cycle routes in the city. Although I have taken part in bike rides from one town to another with many people in the UK, I had never undertaken a guided bike tour of a city before. I enjoy cycling in and around a town as a solitary pursuit and don't like to ride in a peloton – a cycling pack. I have a better sense of direction when riding a bike in an unfamiliar town than when I am walking through it.

Some fellow-cyclists had already gathered at the departure point, a cycle storage place inside a Munich train station, when we arrived to go on a tour of the city. All the bikes were roughly the same size but the height of each saddle was adjusted according to the height of the rider – it was pulled up very high on the bike hired by Derek. We were led by a local German lady who spoke to everyone in English. She instructed our group of twenty or so participants to trail one another rather than riding side by side so that we didn't obstruct the traffic in the town. Being taller and hence more visible than everyone else in the group, Derek was assigned the job of riding at the back so the guide could ensure that no one in the group was lost.

We then cycled through the town to get to the English Garden, which had been laid out two centuries ago. I wondered if the Nazis wanted to change its name since they would have found it spooky to have an English garden in their backyard. Unlike the Tiergarten in Berlin, it was known by its descriptive name and called Ein Englischer Garten. I asked the tour guide if its name had stayed the same during the Nazi era and she said that so far as she knew it had remained unchanged. The park, which has a river and a few rivulets flowing through it, looks a very rural landscape in the middle of the city. The guide told us that the idea was to design a romantic park in the heart of Munich where one could, if one wanted, sit on a bench and compose a poem. It had taken an American-born British physicist, Benjamin Thompson, to design such a park in Munich.

It was very pleasant around mid-morning but there weren't many people in the park. Derek told me that a lot of people come there, usually in the afternoon. As we reached a Chinese tower inside the English Garden – modelled on the one in Kew Gardens – our guide asked us to lock our bikes and stop for some refreshments at a nearby beer garden. Derek fancied a cold beer and I ordered an apple strudel with a coffee.

The first time I ever ate an apple strudel was at a German bakery in Srinagar run by a German woman who had married a Kashmiri man. It was called 'Glocken Bakery' – our foreign language tutor once told us that Glocken meant 'a bell' in English. The German woman also sold cheese cake at her bakery and when I saw someone buying a slice, I was surprised that cheese could be used as the main ingredient in the baking of a cake. The bakery was popular with foreign tourists visiting Srinagar in the days when the town was peaceful.

Derek told me something about a beer garden in Munich. "It's the biggest of its kind in the world. In fact, one of the reasons I moved to Munich in the first place is the quality of beer served in this town. I prefer to drink beer in a garden rather than a beer-hall because I love being outdoors. I walked a lot through the parks in London. My face and arms became so tanned that my friends believed I'd just come back from sunning myself on a beach holiday."

The seed cones of hop plants are used by brewers around the world to flavour their beer. Since alcohol consumption is prohibited in Islam, hops were grown semi-secretly as a cash crop in Kashmir during my childhood and its farms were usually surrounded by apple orchards to hide them from visiting townspeople. I once caught a glimpse of one such small hops farm inside a vast orchard. The farm was fenced by iron mesh, the top of which had wires running across it. Rows of hop plants were connected to the wires to hold them upright. The produce of these farms was sent to breweries outside Kashmir. My grandfather told me that our deposed Maharaja had a brewery at his palace in Srinagar that was fed by a mountain stream. It is known as 'Alcohol Stream', a name that evoked in my mind's eye a fantastical world in which people got intoxicated just by drinking from the stream.

This elusive mountain stream also transported me to the underworld of Hades through which the river Lethe flows, making anyone drinking from it forgetful. The only brewery I ever saw was near the port of Hamburg. I sometimes walked past its windows and marvelled at the enormous shiny copper kettles inside the building.

Our refreshment break over, it was time to hit the saddle again. Derek resisted the temptation of having a second jug of beer lest he become tipsy and our tour guide lose sight of him. When we reached the edge of the English Garden, everyone got off their bikes to watch three or four surfers riding a wave on the River Eisbach one by one. I had heard about surfers riding a river wave in the English Garden but I was puzzled as to how a river could produce a wave high enough for surfing until I saw the water gushing from an underground canal with such force that it created a constant wave. The tour guide pointed out that it was a man-made phenomenon.

I asked Derek about the Olympic Park in Munich and he said it was located at the outskirts of town. I could only remember, having seen it so many times in my childhood, the picture of the American swimmer Mark Spitz, sporting a thick moustache, who had won seven gold medals in the Munich Olympics in 1972. It was many years later that I learnt about the kidnapping of eleven Israeli athletes at the venue and a calamitous rescue effort that resulted in such extreme bloodshed that Mark Spitz, being Jewish, had feared for his own safety. It was quite by chance that I met the person who eventually broke Mark Spitz's Olympic record, Mike Phelps, when we hosted him for a couple of nights in the hotel where I work.

After we finished our cycling tour Derek obliged me by asking to meet him again the next day in Marienplatz. I took a train there in the afternoon and found a group of teenagers sitting in a circle waving EU flags. As I got nearer, I discovered that these youngsters were listening rapturously to Beethoven's 9th Symphony played through portable speakers. It stopped me in my tracks. A man passing by gave each of them an approving pat on the shoulder. It was only when I noticed that the teenagers were sitting in front of an enclosed area displaying two or three banners bearing the name 'Pegida', a German far-right political movement, that I realised what was happening: waving EU flags was the teenagers' way of protesting peacefully against Pegida. Later, I learned that the 9th Symphony is the anthem of the European Union. Half a dozen spectators who looked like vagrants – I assumed they were Pegida sympathizers – were sitting on chairs inside the enclosure, perhaps waiting for a representative of their party to arrive. A few policemen stood nearby guarding the enclosure.

I found Derek waiting for me in the square and we walked along looking for a table outside a coffee-shop. What did Derek think about Pegida activists making speeches in Marienplatz? Derek said that he wasn't bothered much by Pegida but it was the rise of the AfD (Alternative für Deutschland) political party that really worried him. In the early 1980s Derek had sought refuge in Germany from the authoritarian communist regime in Poland. "Hundreds and thousands of refugees arrived in Germany after the War, mostly ethnic Germans driven out of Poland and other countries. I'm glad I left Britain before the EU referendum took place. Living in Germany means living in the heart of the European Union and I can take a coach or train to nine different countries surrounding Germany. I can never forget the time of the Iron Curtain when you couldn't cross from Poland into Germany." After Derek had moved to Germany, he was unable to return to Krakow to see his parents for many years. "I strongly disagree with those of my countrymen who are dead against accepting a share of the refugees arriving in the EU. A lot of them are resentful about the ownership of the media in Poland by German companies. Incredibly, some people still believe that their government in Poland is run by Jews."

Derek had decided to move back to Krakow because Poland is now a member of the EU and he is free to travel to any EU country when he returns to his home-town. He felt that Poland had benefited greatly from its membership of the EU. I asked him if he was going to visit London again in the future. "I still have an account in Lloyds Bank in London and I'd like to spend my savings in touring Britain again after my retirement," he said. He likes the English seaside and often took a train from London on excursions there when he lived in the UK.

I wanted to know if Derek had been to Marienplatz the day before to see his favourite team, Bayern Munich, celebrating their win. "Of course, I was here," Derek enthused. He'd sometimes worn a Bayern Munich cap in London. I mentioned the incident I'd witnessed of a man sporting an England cap who was harassed at the train station. Derek said that he had never worn a Bayern Munich cap when he went to see his favourite team in England playing a match at The Den in Bermondsey. He questioned the judgement of the England fan but at the same time felt sorry that he was harassed.

I asked Derek jokingly if he had yet found a new girlfriend in Munich. "In fact I have," he said with a glint in his eye. I commented that I thought he was going to refrain from starting a new relationship since he was planning to lead a quiet life in Krakow. Derek informed me that his new girlfriend was from Poland, was the same age as him and, like him, had a grownup daughter from a previous marriage. Derek felt optimistic about the future of his relationship this time around, especially since she was willing to move back to Poland with him. She came from a small town not far from Krakow and owned a small house there. "We've got many things in common," said Derek. "She's a fan of outdoor activities like walking and loves travelling. Besides she's suffered a great deal like me by going through a lengthy divorce and so we get along very well."

Derek ate out when he lived in London but in Munich he mostly ate at home. He'd brought kilos of sausages with him whenever he came back to London after visiting Krakow. But in Munich he liked the smell of the fresh bread sold at numerous bakeries. "In London you have to go to an exclusive store like Selfridges to buy the artisan loaf that's sold at every bakery in Munich," said Derek. "As I'm diet conscious, I'm eating less sausage meat and more bread since I moved to Munich."

On a stone wall in Marienplatz a tramp displayed several notices, handwritten on multicoloured sheets of paper, stating that Anthony Quinn had told him in 1944 when he was 28 years old that there were only three bad boys in Hollywood, viz. Lee Van Cleef, Lee Marvin and Quinn himself. He sat on a stool guarding this artwork. Also to be seen was a bronze statue of Juliet from Shakespeare's tragic love story mounted on a nearby pedestal gifted to Munich by the city of Verona. The long-necked Juliet is covering one of her breasts with a forearm and I wondered why the other breast looked so polished. It wasn't long before my question was answered: I saw a man reaching out to fondle Juliet's exposed breast. Perhaps he sought her blessing.

Derek told me that there were many students living in Munich, the second largest number of students in Germany after Berlin. The University of Munich wasn't that far from where we sat in Marienplatz. I asked him if I could cruise the river Isar in a riverboat. He laughed and said that I could better cruise the river on a raft since it is very shallow. "Where can I catch a glimpse of the Bavarian Alps?" I asked. He advised that I take a train to Garmisch in the south if I wanted to see the Alps. He offered to show me one of his favourite Bavarian towns, Regensburg, instead. It is a medieval town situated at the confluence of the Danube, Naab and Regen rivers. Regensburg hadn't suffered much damage during World War II and its Old Town has remained intact.

We rushed to the main station to catch a train to Regensburg and were greeted by a staff member of the Deutsche Bahn standing in the foyer of the ticket hall. He issued tickets in no time and handed us a printout of the timetable for our return journey. A train to Regensburg was just about to depart. Derek said that he loves Regensburg because it's a comparatively sleepy little town and he enjoys going there whenever he can.

As the train pulled into the station in Regensburg, I saw a jumble of bikes on the platform, suggesting it was a university town. We headed straight to the river through the Old Town, passing a cathedral known as Dom St Peter. I mentioned to Derek that I recalled having seen a picture of this cathedral with a stone carving on its outside wall of three Jewish men suckling on a female pig. This disconcerting folk art image, he said, was as old as the cathedral itself, which was built in medieval times. But it was only during the Nazi era that schoolchildren were brought to cathedrals like Regensburg to show them such carvings. "I am a Christian but I detest such depictions of Jewish people on church walls," said Derek. He took me inside a smaller church round the corner that is dedicated to John the Baptist. The church was empty and Derek sat on a bench to pray for a few minutes.

We walked across a 12th century stone bridge built over the Danube, Derek's favourite place in Regensburg. I could see a few big riverboats from the bridge, some of which make a stop in Regensburg while cruising on the Danube. The town looked picturesque and there were a few people sitting on the benches of a riverside café soaking up the sun. But we didn't have time to join them and walked hurriedly back to the station to catch a train back to Munich, where I was to gain moving experience of Munich's past.

Capital of the Movement

Nowadays one of the most liveable cities in the world, Munich was once the capital of the Nazi movement. I have always associated Bavaria with the majestic Alps and wasn't fully aware of its role in the birth of Nazism after World War I until I revisited the city. I had read William L. Shirer's voluminous book, *The Rise and Fall of the Third Reich*, when I was young but forgotten much about the history of the Weimar Republic except for the mind-boggling fact that there was such hyperinflation in Germany in the 1920s that at one point in its brief existence people carried money in wheelbarrows to pay for groceries. One of my classmates in Kashmir was often to be seen carrying Shirer's hefty book around and everyone thought he was very studious.

Living in Hamburg for a few months in the early 1990s, I never sought to learn anything about its history either before or during the Third Reich. The interwar years seemed like a distant era to me since I was then only in my early twenties. When I moved to London in the mid-1990s, I often heard people say "Don't mention the war if you're travelling in Germany in case you offend people." It seemed that only

Harry Enfield's comic character, Jürgen, a German in the UK, was eager to talk about the War, to the bewilderment and alarm of his hosts. Had I been acquainted with *Fawlty Towers* at the time, I would also have seen hotelier John Cleese strenuously failing not to mention the war to his outraged German guests.

The lady who'd guided me on a bike tour of the town the day before told me that the post-war period had been traumatic for her parents and it had taken them a long time to come to terms with the past and reconcile to the idea that their own parents' generation had adhered to the Nazi philosophy and joined the party in millions when it came to power in 1933.

Some years ago I read Jorge Luis Borges's story of a fictional Nazi, Otto Dietrich zur Linde, in which the protagonist shows no remorse for his actions on the night before his execution and has no wish to be understood. He speaks of high culture – Brahms, Nietzsche and Shakespeare – and believes that Raskolnikov's murderous undertaking was more difficult than Napoleon's. Zur Linde is sure that mankind is on the threshold of a new age, and that this new age, like the first years of Islam or Christianity, demands new men. It seemed an improbable tale to me until I saw a documentary clip of the Nuremberg trials during which Hermann Goering tries to make a lengthy statement but, forbidden by the judge, then declares himself to be Not Guilty. Goering laughs during the trial and, like Borges' character, shows no remorse. I am usually so unsure with Borges whether I am reading his collected 'fictions' or his 'non-fictions' (Borges is a master storyteller who blurs the line between them) that I have to check the title on the book's cover.

I have always found disturbing the affiliation of a murderous regime with high culture. The Nazis regarded modern artists such as Paul Klee and Pablo Picasso as degenerate and even organised an exhibition of modern art in Munich under the title of 'Degenerate Art.' I couldn't help but find it incredible that a failed artist not only became the leader of the Nazi party but also pronounced judgment on some of the greatest works of contemporary art, declaring them to be despicable.

Before visiting Munich, I hadn't planned to go out of my way to see buildings and squares associated with the Third Reich because I found the prospect forbidding. But now I was here in the city I felt that I had to overcome my nervousness. Setting out on a general tour of Munich several years later, I still felt reluctant to explore the darkest period in its twentieth-century history and it took me a couple of days to decide to join a walking tour specifically of the Third Reich.

I would have preferred our tour guide to be a German whose grandparents had lived in Munich during the War, so as to hear his or her opinion about the inglorious title that the city had earned – 'Hauptstadt der Bewegung' (Capital of the [Nazi] Movement). As it happened, our guide that day was English. He asked the question that was no doubt at the back of the minds of most of the people in his audience: how could the land of Goethe, Schiller, Brahms and Beethoven produce a generation of men and women who hailed the rallying cries of the Nazis? He delved into the immediate aftermath of World War I and the humiliations Germany had suffered at the hands of the Allied powers, who'd demanded reparations from them under the Treaty of Versailles. The terms of the treaty were deemed by many to be too harsh and thus it became instrumental in the downfall of the Weimar Republic.

The guide stated that the people of Germany allowed themselves to be led by a madman whom they mistakenly believed to be their only saviour. The Nazis blamed Jews and Communists for the failures of the Weimar Republic and found a few wealthy donors in Munich who sympathised with their cause. Those wealthy people, he said, were afraid of a Bolshevik revolution and therefore funded the Nazi party.

Our first stop was Königsplatz where the Nazis held their enormous rallies. I had seen a black and white photograph of this square with rays of light radiating from the Swastika at its centre superimposed on the image, which was used for Nazi propaganda. A few old buildings near Königsplatz had survived the War. Although the metal eagles above their entrances were removed after the Nazis were defeated, the swastikas inlaid in the mosaics on the ceiling of their porches have remained intact. An American on our walking tour told me that he hadn't expected to see any swastikas in Munich. He had been to Vietnam a few years ago and was surprised to see swastikas painted on the walls of many temples there and thus came to realize that it was in fact a religious symbol.

The Oxford Concise Dictionary states that the word means 'well-being' in Sanskrit. It became known and loathed worldwide as a symbol of Nazism after they turned it 45 degrees. My tutor in Kashmir taught me to call it 'Hakenkreuz' in German.

Our tour guide showed us the so-called 'Brown House', the head office of the NSDAP during the Third Reich. Membership records of the Nazi party had survived quite by chance, he informed us, since they were sent to a printer to be shredded before American troops reached Munich. The list of party members ran into millions, including doctors and scientists, some of whom remained unrepentant for a long time after the war. It was shocking to learn of the number of doctors who subscribed to such a murderous philosophy. It's well-known that the Americans sent some of the scientists to the USA where they were recruited to work on its space programme.

When I heard the word 'denazification' for the first time, it sounded to me like a clinical term such as 'detoxification'. The Allied initiative to rid German society of Nazi remnants was abandoned after a few years because there were so many of them that it would have been impossible to send all of them to prison. And I found it an illuminating incongruity that during the Nuremberg trials the Americans worked hard during the day to prosecute the Nazi leaders and hosted parties at night where everyone drank and danced.

The men and women who experienced the horrors of

war as children in Germany are still haunted by it. But Munich has struggled to come to terms with its past more than any other German city. Our guide told us that Heinrich Himmler's daughter is still living in Munich. We could scarcely believe it when he added that she is a "daddy's girl". When I visited Berlin, someone told me that Wannsee was a wonderful place for walking because of its forests and lakes. But I couldn't bring myself to go there because I knew of the infamous conference held in the town by Nazi officials, including Himmler's top deputy, Reinhard Heydrich, to discuss the implementation of the 'Final Solution to the Jewish Question'.

I met a lady named Mrs Eichmann in London a few years ago who told me that every time she checked into a hotel and gave her name, the receptionist would pause and look quizzically at her as if to ask "Any relation to Adolf Eichmann?" "No, I am not a distant relative of Otto Adolf Eichmann," she would say, vexed by the question mark hanging over her name whenever she introduced herself to others. She told me that she had never travelled to America in case her surname caused her to be detained at the airport by an immigration office. "Some people like to change their first name," she said, "but I've always wanted to change my last name."

Adolf Eichmann escaped to Argentina after the war using a false name but was captured by Mossad and brought to Tel Aviv to be put on trial. Derek had told me about an Argentine town in the foothills of the Andes called Bariloche that resembled Munich because many Nazis had escaped there and built Munich-style homes. Borges was bothered by the presence of Nazi sympathisers in his country. He had leaned towards the Allies in his writings but also felt sorry about the fate of the German nation. As a result, he was offered a job as a poultry inspector to cause him embarrassment. My friend Derek also told me about the arrest in Bariloche of Erich Priebke, a Nazi war criminal who'd lived there comfortably for fifty years and worked as a schoolteacher.

The guide showed us the building where members of the German Workers' Party, which became the Nazi party, used to meet in its early days. "It's beyond belief," he said, "how a man with a toothbrush moustache could bamboozle millions into joining his party." The red clothbound membership book of the NSDAP looks like a contemporary German passport except for an eagle insignia and a swastika printed on it in gold ink. The use of the word 'socialist' in the official name of the Nazi party had bothered me as a teenager. I understood later that it was in fact the Nazi fascination with nationalism that had made it such an extremely dangerous philosophy, even a religion of sorts. Our English guide read out a long list of people who had shown faith in the Nazi movement from the very beginning, sometimes using the words 'Nazi' and 'a believer' in the same sentence.

The people who joined the Nazi party at its inception were at the top of the list during the post-war denazification drive since they were considered to be true believers. Many people had joined the party in later years in order to get Nazi government contracts for the supply of goods and services to feed the war machinery. Factories were run around the clock and many of them relied on slave labour to churn out Messerschmitt aircraft as if they were producing pushbikes. Britain was the first country to industrialise during the 19th Century, producing a quarter of the total industrial output in the world. But a hundred years later it was Germany, eager to establish its own empire, that used its factories to make tanks and fighter planes. The Allied powers wanted German industrial capacity to be reduced after World War II so that the country couldn't indulge such an ambition again. But there was an unexpected economic revival (the so-called 'economic miracle') in post-war Germany and the country has become an industrial powerhouse at the helm of a European Union that started as a peace project after the war.

As we walked around Munich, someone in our group asked the guide if there was much resistance to the Nazi movement when it got going in the city. The tour guide cited the example of a small group of students known as White Rose who in 1942 distributed leaflets calling for passive resistance to the Nazi government but were soon arrested and executed by the SS. "The Nazi judges in Munich were very ruthless," he said, "which is why some people like to call the city the Capital of Suppression."

On my maiden voyage to the UK, I sailed from Hamburg to Harwich. One sunny late afternoon I sat on the deck with my nose in a book by V S Naipaul. A German who sat nearby struck up a conversation with me as the ship sailed towards the British Isles, referring to the book I was reading as 'The Empire Strikes Back'. I hadn't heard of this *Star Wars* film at the time but guessed that he was alluding to the British Empire. The Nazis had threatened to establish an empire that would last a thousand years.

Churchill himself made a speech, expressing the hope that the British Empire would last that long, although he believed that the empires of the future would be 'empires of the mind'. But World War II had put paid to his imperial ambitions and a few years after making the speech, the British government recalled the colonials who ruled the Indian subcontinent to rebuild their own war-damaged country. The wartime prime minister warned his countrymen in a famous speech that upon their final battle depended the survival of Christian civilization, thereby showing disdain for the beliefs of the colonized subjects whom he thought incapable of governing themselves.

We gathered around the guide outside a building where the Munich Agreement was signed. The British and French governments handed over a part of Czechoslovakia to the Nazi leader, thus affording him a major victory without fighting a battle. I had seen a photo of this building, taken in 1938, with a Union Jack hanging over its porch and a Nazi metal eagle perched above it. The photo looks ominous. After the agreement was signed, the name 'Munich' came to be synonymous with yielding to the demands of a dictator and remained so until the slaughter of Israeli athletes at the 1972 Munich Olympics gave it another negative connotation. Today the building, designed by Paul Troost as the 'Führerbau', is used for teaching music.

The next stop on the tour was another building designed by Troost – a monumental edifice of Nazi architecture used to display the German art that was deemed superior to the 'degenerate' art of so many modern artists. When this building, known as 'Haus der Kunst' (House of Art), opened in October 1939 there was much pomp and pageantry in the town to celebrate two millennia of German art. The War had already started, just a month before, with the German invasion of Poland, but there were many celebrations in the town, including one staged in the English Garden. It was a show of apparent German supremacy over other races and many people turned up in their best attire to salute the Führer. The tour guide told us that some amateur cameramen had captured the celebrations of that day in colour film and that it's surreal to see this documentary film because it looks as if it had been shot only yesterday – a feeling I was able to confirm when I saw it later myself.

Our walking tour ended in Odeonsplatz where Nazis gathered on the 9th of November each year during the Third Reich to commemorate their failed Putsch of 1923. On the 7th November 1938, Herschel Grynszpan, a 17-year-old Polish Jew hiding in Paris, entered the German embassy and shot a diplomat attached to the embassy. Some say that he acted out of despair over the fate of his parents, who'd been deported from Germany, while others claim that he was of unsound mind. This event became the pretext for launching a violent pogrom against the Jews of Germany. On the 9th November many synagogues were burnt and thousands of businesses smashed and looted all over Germany after the Reich Minister of Propaganda, Joseph Goebbels, addressed a crowd near the Odeonsplatz. This has come to be known as Kristallnacht or The Night of Broken Glass.

Having grown up in strife-torn Kashmir, I know how fragile peace can be as I witnessed the smashing of windows as a child in my home-town of Srinagar. It was a terrifying experience for me to see the windows of people's homes broken – sometimes by the police, sometimes by mobs. As a teenager, I summoned up courage one day and asked an adolescent boy why he had thrown a stone that broke our window. He retorted that if I didn't keep quiet he'd break another one and I realised it was a mistake to try telling him to mend his ways. Sometimes paramilitary troops broke the windows of the houses in Srinagar with their batons to silence an angry mob, who, when they got their chance, would break the windows of police stations and other government buildings. My aunt lived in a big family house overlooking a public square in Srinagar and the windows of that house got broken whenever there was a fight between the police and the protestors. However, the windows of my aunt's bedroom, which was on the first floor, miraculously remained intact most of the time. My aunt's mother-in-law always believed that the men who broke the windows of her house knew the exact location of my aunt's bedroom and spared it damage since they hailed from the neighbourhood where the parents of my aunt lived.

Kristallnacht was the prelude to the large-scale destruction of Jewish businesses and property in Germany. It wasn't the fact of Jewish people living segregated lives that was a thorn in Nazi flesh so much as it was their assimilation, which they claimed was making German blood impure. Therefore marriages between Jews and Christians were banned and laws were passed to make the Third Reich free of Jews ('Judenrein'). It was after Kristallnacht that Jews were sent to concentrations camps for their religious persuasion rather than for being socialists or communists, though of course the latter were victimised too.

Before we parted company, our guide informed us that the first concentration camp was set up by the Nazis just outside Munich and advised those of us who were staying in town for another day to go to see it.

A French friend who has lived in Munich for some time had warned me that there is a spirit of heaviness hanging in the air in Dachau. So I wasn't at all sure that I would visit the concentration camp, which is also known as The Academy of Terror, before I travelled to Munich. When I lived in Hamburg for a few months in 1990, I had shunned its Third Reich history and didn't know until many years later that carpet bombing by the Allies had killed more than 40,000 people in the city. Having toured Munich on foot, I now decided, at the behest of the English tour guide, to visit Dachau.

A few people had already gathered outside the tour company's office, waiting for a guide who was running late. He seemed distraught when he arrived and explained that he was late because someone had attempted suicide by jumping on the railway track while he was waiting for a train at the station near his home. The Irishman who was going to be our guide that day resembled the tutor in Kashmir who'd taught me basic German, a man with blonde hair who was known by the name of the foreign language he taught. The tour guide said it wasn't the first time he'd heard of someone killing himself in Munich by jumping onto the rail tracks.

We followed him to a platform at the main station to catch a train to Dachau while he chatted to two or three Americans in the group and I overheard him saying that he was an archaeologist by training. There was an angry-looking old man at the station who gave us a dirty look. The guide said that he knew him. He'd been a fighter pilot during the Third Reich and didn't at all like the idea of him taking groups of people to see a concentration camp site.

We got off the train at Dachau and boarded a bus to the camp. The other people who boarded the bus asked the driver if it was going to the camp and he nodded his head silently.

The guide told us that these days it's expensive to live in Dachau, a somewhat troubling fact considering that its name will forever be associated with its infamous concentration camp. Who would choose to live here? "I knew a few people living in the town," the guide said, "and they told me that when they travel, if anybody asks them where they live they give the name of Munich rather than Dachau so that no one will ask them any awkward questions, like how far they live from the camp?"

Everybody in the bus got off outside the camp and our tour guide gave some advice: "Don't ask me to take a picture of any of you inside the camp and don't take selfies, out of respect for the thousands who perished there."

There is a bookshop inside a glass building surrounded by concrete columns at the entrance of the camp. As we stood at a distance from it, listening to the guide, it struck me that the entrance with its segmented arch and watchtower above it looked similar to that of Auschwitz, except that there were no railway tracks here. I learnt later that the building at the entrance is known as Jourhouse. Both Dachau and Auschwitz were abandoned sites – the former an ammunitions factory and the latter an army barracks – before being turned into a concentration camp (Dachau) and an extermination camp (Auschwitz).

The gate with the words 'Arbeit Macht Frei' wrought in iron became visible as we walked towards the Jourhouse. I had tried to make sense of those three words when I was learning German in Kashmir and wondered for a long time how wretched forced labour could set someone free, thinking that 'Kaput durch Arbeit' would have been more appropriate for such a cruel place. Our guide pointed out that not so long ago the gate, complete with its slogan, had been stolen. It was eventually located when police discovered an attempt to smuggle it across the Norwegian border. "It's astonishing," he said, "how far some people will go to lay their hands on Nazi memorabilia."

As you enter the camp, you are immediately struck by its vastness. Pictures of the camp don't capture the depth of its field like the naked eye. It was a bright day and the white gravel of the empty square reflected the sun. The only sound you could hear was that of the footsteps on gravel of the intrepid souls who had decided to visit the camp that day.

Our Irish guide pointed out that concentration camps weren't the invention of the Nazis but were used by the British in the Boer War before them. Dachau, the first Nazi concentration camp, was established as early as 1933, just a few months after Nazis came to power. The Dachau camp is known as The Academy of Terror because it served as a model for the camps that followed. It was set up by the SS, who ran a training centre just outside the camp. Himmler, the head of the SS, visited the camp in 1936 with his daughter.

The camp at Dachau was initially established for political prisoners like Social Democrats, Communists and trade unionists, and Jewish prisoners were sent to the camp later. Two truckloads of prisoners were sent once or twice a week to Hartheim Castle to be killed by poison gas. I thought it incredible when, by way of explaining the meaning of the phrase 'gift gas', my tutor in Kashmir told me that the word for poison in German is 'gift'. Our guide told us that SS doctors had used some of the prisoners for medical experiments. During the 12 years of Dachau camp's existence more than 40,000 prisoners perished before it was liberated by American troops in April 1945. To get a sense of the horrors of concentration camp life, visitors to the camp these days follow the path taken by those prisoners.

We entered a white building that stretches to the far end of the camp and is used as an exhibition hall. It is known as the Maintenance Building. An American couple at a counter by its entrance were enquiring about the archive of the camp records. They told the lady behind the counter that their relatives had died at the camp and they wanted to find out more about them. The lady was helpful to the couple, who were clearly making an effort to hold back their tears.

Walking slowly towards the other end of this long exhibition hall, I saw an election poster of the NSDAP from 1932 stating 'OUR LAST HOPE…' followed by the name of the party leader who would drag his country into a moral abyss and become responsible for the hopelessness of the millions sent to concentration camps during the Nazi era. The exhibition recreates the path trodden by two hundred thousand prisoners who entered this camp through its iron gate. Nothing prepares a visitor for walking in their path and seeing the horrors of concentration camp life with one's own eyes. The prisoners were stripped of all of their belongings as soon as they entered this building and were given a striped uniform with a number written on it.

There were so many groups of people inside the exhibition hall that it was very noisy and each guide herded their own group into a corner so that they could be heard. Our guide showed us the area in the building where the SS men tied prisoners' hands behind their backs with a chain and then hung them by a hook on a pole. This form of severe punishment often damaged the wrists and the shoulders of the prisoners. One of the Americans in our group was so distressed to hear it that he asked the guide why the Nazis didn't kill their political opponents outright rather than keep them alive in a concentration camp. The guide sighed. "When the Nazis built the first concentration camp in Dachau," he said, "they thought of it as a permanent institution of the Nazi state. There's an inscription on the roof of this building that reads 'There is one path to freedom. Its milestones are: obedience, orderliness and love of fatherland.' In other words, they wanted to discipline, re-educate and then release their prisoners – duly converted to the Nazi creed. As for 'love of fatherland', in the end it was not only Germans who were incarcerated, of course. The man who had asked our guide the question murmured "What a twisted philosophy."

The guide also showed us a wooden bench in the hall on which prisoners were made to kneel in order to be whipped. The American soldiers destroyed these torture benches after they liberated the camp. Also on display is a wheelbarrow, used by the prisoners to carry loads while working as slave labourers and later to carry fellow prisoners who were too weak to walk because of starvation.

The guide pointed to the vast empty square and said it was used for roll call. There was a period when 40,000 prisoners attended this assembly twice a day. He pointed out the grass verges are known as death strips because the prison guards shot dead whoever strayed from the roll call square. The SS doctors carried out medical experiments on the prisoners by freezing them to death to see how long they had got to rescue their soldiers if they were shot down in the English Channel.

Our group was led into another building known as a Bunker in which prisoners who were considered rebellious were locked up in small cells. Another building was used to lock up the clergymen who objected to the Nazi regime. The rest of the clergy in the country had submitted to the authority of the NSDAP. A wall in the narrow yard between these two buildings where the clergymen were executed still shows the bullet marks.

There are three or four newly built houses overlooking the camp. Someone asked our guide what kind of people lived at such close quarters to a concentration camp in which thousands had been tortured and died. The guide said that he had no idea why anyone would build a new house next to a place that weighs so heavily on the conscience of humanity.

It was the sight of the crematorium at the rear of the

camp that everyone in our group found most moving. The oven doors have been left open with metal stretchers placed inside them. The guide told us that these ovens were in operation day and night, burning the corpses of those who died in the camp. Corpses were still piled up high when the Americans entered the camp. There is a building called Barrack X opposite the crematorium that has a high chimney rising from it and a gas chamber fitted inside. The guide pointed to one of the missing shower-heads and said that it could have been stolen by a collector of Nazi memorabilia. Surprisingly, there is no evidence that these particular gas chambers were themselves ever used for killing, but extermination camps were set up elsewhere to kill men and women on an unimaginable scale. I was astonished to see the size of the camp at Dachau but the guide informed us that Auschwitz is far bigger.

Near this crematorium, on the way out, there is a metal sculpture of an unknown prisoner that bears on its pedestal an inscription in German: 'To honour the dead, to warn the living.' Thinking about it, I left the camp in a sombre mood. Were those warning signals I thought I heard? Surely not today...

West-East Divan

I flew to Frankfurt the day after what was officially the busiest day of the year for air travel to and from the UK. Conditions were less crowded when I took an early flight from Heathrow. We landed at Terminal 2 in Frankfurt but I needed to catch a train to the city from Terminal 1. The shuttle bus from this terminal to the other was signposted and a few people stood at the bus stop waiting for the arrival of the next bus. The traffic outside the terminal was at a standstill. I waited for half an hour for the cars and taxis to move and then went back inside the terminal to see if I could find an alternative way to get to Terminal 1.

An assistant at the airport directed me to a train platform on the upper level of the building where I could catch a shuttle train. The train doors were wide open and it was packed tight with people waiting for it to depart. But the doors stayed open for quite a while until the train driver asked everyone to get off the train and catch a shuttle bus instead. Some of the passengers were clearly exasperated and I overheard a woman telling her companion that this kind of thing was why she didn't like Frankfurt. But I wasn't in a rush and took the delay without annoyance.

The vehicles outside the terminal hadn't moved an inch. Motorists and taxi drivers were losing their temper and shouting at each other. It was the first time that I'd seen such a chaotic situation at an airport in Germany, the opposite of the orderliness one usually finds on arrival in the country. But the words uttered by the tour guide in Munich – '*ordnung muss sein*' (there must be order) – when trying to explain the German national psyche to us, were still buzzing in my head. So it was with a kind of relief that I witnessed a semblance of chaos on my arrival in Frankfurt. During my previous visits to the country, I'd found that many people in Germany were highly strung. Perhaps it was because of their desire to do things perfectly that they became so easily agitated. When I tried to ask a lady a question in a tourist office in Munich while she was booking an online ticket for me she stated that she 'must' focus on booking the ticket to get it right and then she'd answer.

On my first visit to Germany in the late 1980s, I had wondered why Bonn was the capital of West Germany when everyone travelling to the country from abroad arrived in Frankfurt. I learnt later that Frankfurt had in fact been the seat of the German Bundestag for 50 years from 1816 and was thus the capital of Germany. Bonn and Frankfurt may both have been valid claimants but the title of capital went to Bonn after World War II. Some say that the first post-war Chancellor preferred the town of Bonn as the capital because it was close to his home-town. At any rate, Frankfurt, already a financial centre, became an international airline hub. It is probably of all European cities the one that looks most American, thanks to the abundance of skyscrapers at its centre.

It eventually took me an hour and a half to travel between the two terminals at Frankfurt airport. The city itself seemed very quiet on this weekend afternoon in comparison to the crowd at the airport. Someone told me that the city was so quiet because school holidays in the State of Hesse had already started.

I had stayed in Frankfurt for a night a few years earlier. The walk from my hotel to the main train station amid the towering skyscrapers had transported me again to Lang's *Metropolis*. I had stood outside the Messe building, which the people of Frankfurt sarcastically call 'The Pencil' because of its cylindrical structure and pointed top. The cars on the road sped past but there were hardly any people walking on the pavement.

On the way to the train station at that time I saw a high-rise building which had a big blue metal Euro sign mounted on stainless steel tubes on its front lawn – the sign featured yellow stars signifying the member countries of the eurozone monetary union.

The location of the Eurotower, as it is known, in Willy-Brandt-Platz reminded me of a picture of the former Social Democrat Chancellor, after whom the square was named, kneeling at a war memorial in Warsaw in 1970 to show penance for the victims of the Warsaw Ghetto Uprising during the war.

As a student in Kashmir, I had cut out this historic photo from a magazine and pinned it to a notice board in my study. I'd been very moved by the words of Willy Brandt describing that moment: 'As I stood on the edge of Germany's historical abyss, feeling the burden of millions of murders, I did what people do when words fail.'

The European Central Bank, or ECB, has now got a new home in a polygonal double tower that some people call 'Debit and Credit'. There were protests by anti-capitalists against the austerity measures in many European countries when the new ECB building opened its doors in 2015. The building is located in the east end of town whereas bankers in Frankfurt mostly live in the so-called 'Westend'. Having assumed that East End and West End were exclusively extremities of the City of London, I was surprised to find a Westend district in Frankfurt.

I took a train to Westend station, which has an ornate pillar covered in a mosaic at its centre. It was empty at the weekend. I came out of the station to find a side-street lined with elegant apartment blocks. I was going to meet Reza, whom I had known in London for many years. He worked as a banker in Frankfurt and lived in an apartment in the Westend. He insisted that we meet at his home rather than a coffee-shop.

When I met Reza for the first time in London, he was a trainee banker. He was attending for a few months a training course organised by the Deutsche Bank in the hotel where I work. He had asked me to arrange a bouquet for his fiancée in Frankfurt, with a message consisting of a couplet from the *Divan-e-Hafez*, a collection by the 14th century Persian poet Hafez. Reza told me that his fiancée, Rifka, liked Goethe and was familiar with Hafez's poems through Goethe's translation, *West-östlicher Divan*. He had met his fiancée at a cultural exchange programme in Iran.

Both of Reza's parents were doctors who had worked in two or three different countries before settling in London. Reza was a graduate of a business school in London, selected by the Deutsche Bank to work for them. He was good with numbers and was therefore recruited by a German bank as soon as he graduated from business school. He grew up in a liberal home and his parents had encouraged him to follow his own path rather than their footsteps and become a doctor. He preferred Economics, the subject that had led him to apply for a job in the banking sector. But he considered his work for a big international bank as a pact with the devil in exchange for knowledge, like Goethe's Faust. Reza wanted to work for the Deutsche Bank to learn how the global financial system worked. He had told me when he was a trainee that he aimed to work for an international bank for a few years to make some money and then intended to give up his job.

Reza joined Deutsche Bank in 2003 and had risen quickly to become a manager just before the financial crisis of 2008 that caused the shake-up of many banks, including the Deutsche Bank, and he lost his job. He had made plenty of money in five years but he'd also got into the habit of spending it quickly like other bankers in the City of London. Reflecting on his first few years as a banker, Reza said it had been a roller-coaster ride. I had once seen him with some Asian friends of his from New York in a hotel bar in London. They were bragging to the barman that they had made a cool million two days before and wanted to spend some of the money drinking expensive champagne. Their lips were chapped because they had been continuously drinking in the bar for two days and were applying lip balm at regular intervals. The drinking of Dom Perignon from morning till evening had rung alarm bells in the head of the bar manager, whose monthly salary was less than the amount on the New York bankers' bar bill for a day, and he had phoned American Express to check if the credit card they were using was actually their own. When I saw him there, Reza was visibly embarrassed by the drunken stupor of his friends. They had ordered a limo to go to a gentleman's club later that night but the limo driver brought them back to the hotel after half an hour, complaining that they had fallen asleep in the back of the limo and he couldn't wake them up.

Reza and Rifka had married in 2006. Rifka's father is an Iranian Jew and her mother a German Christian. Both Reza's parents are Iranian – his father a Muslim and mother a Zoroastrian. Rifka was closer to her father's family and had travelled to Iran a few times to meet them. Born in Frankfurt, she doesn't speak Farsi but understands the meaning of many words when her father converses with his relatives. Her grandmother is in her nineties but sprightly for her age.

I had met Rifka with Reza in London when they were engaged. Rifka had striking curly red hair. Reza told me that she got on well with his parents and both of them were fond of her. They hosted a lavish wedding in a Park Lane hotel for his son and some of the couple's relatives had travelled from Iran to attend the wedding in London. Reza had hired a yacht for his honeymoon in St Tropez. "It was what other bankers did in those days," Reza said, "and I tried to keep up with them." When Reza was made redundant in 2008, he was without a job for almost a year. His parents supported him financially during those months. Reza said that he was told not to be risk averse when he was training as a banker but he has been cautious ever since he lost his job. He works now for a smaller bank in Frankfurt, which is involved in developmental work around the world. Reza said that 14 years after making a pact with the devil, he was still in his grip. "I wanted to let the devil go but it's the devil who wont let me go," he told me wistfully.

Reza lives in a spacious three-bedroom flat in Frankfurt. He is renting the flat as he can't afford to buy such a flat in the Westend. Rifka works as a schoolteacher. And they have a six-year-old daughter called Mahsa, which means 'like the moon' in Farsi. I asked Reza about his move from London to Frankfurt. He told me that when he lost his job in the City of London, it had shaken him to the core. So he decided to leave the UK and come to live in Frankfurt as soon as he found a job in Germany. "Frankfurt has got a long association with banking, which is why some people like to call it Bankfurt."

I asked Reza about his experience during the banking crisis of 2008. He said that he understood why people have little sympathy for the bankers. He had lived an extravagant life as a banker for quite a few years before the crisis and knew his superiors earned an obscene amount of money.

"Frankfurt is the city where the Rothschild family started their banking dynasty," he told me. "It was because financiers like the Rothschilds happened to be Jewish that some people thought Jews were responsible for the financial crisis. The family was involved in the Napoleonic wars by way of lending money but the world of banking has changed a bit in the last two hundred years." I recalled that a Frenchman working with me in 2008 told me every day that Jews had pulled the plug and caused the crisis, and this was even though its biggest casualty was the Lehman Brothers – an investment bank started by the son of a Jewish merchant. I couldn't take him seriously since he believed in all kinds of conspiracy theories.

Reza was glad that he'd found a job in a different bank. "Deutsche Bank hasn't fully recovered from the financial shock of 2008 and the bank has laid off more employees recently to cut its payroll further. Sure, Frankfurt is the home of the Deutsche Bank but I prefer to work for a smaller bank here." He avoids the adjoining Taunusanlage Park because he doesn't want to see the shiny twin towers of his former employer at close quarters.

I wanted to know how well Reza had settled in Frankfurt after working in the City of London for several years. He said that Frankfurt's reputation as a boring city isn't completely unmerited. Although he was born in Iran, he grew up in London – culturally a far more interesting place to live than Frankfurt. Whereas Munich has an English Garden, however, Frankfurt has got an English theatre. Reza has learnt German since he moved to Frankfurt but he still likes to go to The English Theatre, which is the largest of its kind in continental Europe.

Since the city hosts many big international trade fairs, Frankfurt is a more transient kind of place where people arrive from other countries for a few days to exhibit their wares and then leave town without actually seeing much of it. The area around the Messe Tower feels desolate when there are no trade fairs.

Reza had been to a book fair there and found it too big for his liking. I attended a book fair in London a few years ago and felt overwhelmed by the crowd there. I was waiting in line in a coffee-shop when a white-bearded man standing in front of me in the queue, who looked in his wide-brimmed hat like Walt Whitman, commented on the number of people waiting to buy tea or coffee by saying that during the gold rush the only people who made money were those who sold shovels. He revealed that he was a small publisher and exhibited at the fair.

I stayed in a high-rise hotel near Messe Tower and had in fact seen its illuminated sign on top of the building from the airplane on my previous visit before it landed at Frankfurt airport. Now, years later, I was allocated a room on a very high floor of the same building, a good vantage point for seeing the city. The sun setting behind the hills painted the horizon in warm colours and when I woke up in the morning I found that the city had been washed by the rain in the night and there were white clouds hanging over the uplands. Frankfurt is actually quite a small city compared to other financial capitals like London and New York. I could see the edges of the city dissolving into green fields from my hotel window – the city looks more hospitable when seen from above than it does looking at the skyscrapers from ground level.

It was a sunny afternoon and Reza wanted to show me Frankfurt's skyline from its river, so we took a walk to an iron bridge to catch a boat. It is a pedestrian bridge and Reza said he crossed it often to walk to the other side of town. He pointed to an inscription in Greek on top of the bridge and said that he was baffled by it for a long time until he found out it was from Homer's *Odyssey* and meant

'Sailing over the wine-dark sea,

Unto men of strange speech.'

Reza feels somehow attuned to these words, he told me, since he knows it's an age-old desire for men and women to cross waters and meet people from other cultures who speak different languages. I remarked in an earlier chapter that people had put padlocks with romantic messages on a door in what remained of the Berlin Wall. Here also, I saw padlocks with romantic messages tied to the wrought-iron railings of the bridge, only in this case the messages had been meticulously, probably professionally, engraved.

A boat was docked at the pier when we walked back

over the bridge and we boarded it at once as it was about to depart. The boat sailed in the direction of the port in Frankfurt. The river Main, which joins the Rhine a few miles from Frankfurt, is canalized, like the nearby Neckar that flows through Heidelberg.

The glass towers in the centre of Frankfurt reflected the afternoon sun as Reza named the towers of various banks for me. The boat turned back near the port where sea-containers could be seen piled up on one bank of the river. The boat docked again near the iron bridge and picked up a few more people for the second leg of the cruise. As it approached another footbridge over the Main, a tannoy informed us that it was designed by the architect, Albert Speer Jnr. Reza told me that the architect's firm was based in Frankfurt though the State of Berlin didn't want him to work on a project in their city because of his father's association with the Third Reich.

I asked Reza about the half-timbered houses in Frankfurt that I'd seen depicted on vintage postcards. He said that most of the town was razed to the ground during the war and the Wehrmacht had even blown up the iron bridge near which we had boarded the boat. The bridge had been rebuilt after the war. A few of the half-timbered houses opposite the town hall had also been rebuilt and they are one of the main tourist attractions in the town.

Rifka was going to show me Goethe's house, so we waited for her in a café near the town hall. The medieval building of the town hall, Reza said, was used for the coronation of the German emperors, which is perhaps why Queen Elizabeth II made a stop there when she visited the city in 2015. Rifka arrived punctually to walk us to Goethe's house. I had spent much time in the reading room of the Goethe-Institut in Delhi and this was an opportunity at last to see the home of the great literary figure who had lent his name to this significant cultural organisation.

A poet living down the road where I had rented a room in Hampstead in the mid-1990s gave me his dog-eared copy of Goethe's *Selected Verse* one day and it was this book that acquainted me with Suleika and Hatem in *Divan-e-Hafez*. It wasn't until two decades after reading Goethe's poem that I learnt it was in fact written by Marianne Jung, who had become such an inspiration for the poet that he called Marianne his Suleika and himself Hatem – a legendary generous person in Kashmiri folklore. Goethe was a statesman as well as a poet, playwright, novelist, painter and scientist. He was opposed to the French Revolution and fought in a battle against Napoleon. Borges says Goethe was a tolerant person, a man who greeted Napoleon when Napoleon invaded Germany. In that respect he was opposite to those Germans who were so easily roused to fanaticism during the Third Reich. In fact, Napoleon Bonaparte was an admirer of Goethe's work and liked his novel, *Sorrows of Young Werther*, which is why Goethe's home in Weimar was spared destruction.

On our way to the Goethe House, Rifka showed me the church where a national assembly was held in 1848 to debate plans for a unified Germany. She also showed me Frankfurt's own Bridge of Sighs near the St Paul's Church. In Venice it was the prisoners who sighed while walking over the bridge that connected the interrogation rooms to a prison, whereas it was the wealthy merchants of Frankfurt who exhaled a deep breath while crossing the Bridge of Sighs after having paid taxes in one of the wings of the city hall.

When we reached Goethe House, Rifka met a Russian friend who guided small groups on walking tours of Frankfurt. She told us that she had dropped this landmark building from her English-speaking tour because many of the people who joined this tour asked her who Johann Wolfgang Goethe was and she felt utterly deflated by such a question.

The black-painted door of Goethe's family home has a wrought-iron panel above it with the initials of Goethe's father, 'JCG' (for Johann Casper Goethe) painted in gold. The original house was destroyed during the war and it has been painstakingly rebuilt. It doesn't look that big from the outside but when you walk in and see its opulent interior, it becomes apparent that Goethe's father was a wealthy man. Near a grand staircase leading to the upper floors a lady staff member handed us a copy of the layout of the house, then recommended we start at the top floor and make our way down. We climbed up the stairs to reach the top floor and found a toy theatre in one of the rooms there. Given to young Goethe when he was only four years old, it had inspired him to write plays when he grew up. Another room, known as the

Writing Room, displays a desk on which Goethe wrote the first version of *Faust*. An adjacent room charts Goethe's life from his birth to the writing of this, the great work of his life.

On the second floor is the room where Goethe is believed to have been born. The rooms of his mother and sister are on the same floor. The other two rooms consist of a picture gallery and a library. Goethe's father was an art collector and the books in the library belonged to him. Goethe's mentor, Herder, had introduced him to the works of Shakespeare. I had found no library in Shakespeare's home when I visited Stratford-upon-Avon in 2005. I was surprised when I heard some people in England calling Dante Alighieri 'the Italian Shakespeare,' given that he was born three centuries before the birth of the Bard. I've not heard anyone in Italy calling Shakespeare 'the English Dante'.

The house next door to the Goethe House is a museum that displays paintings selected to familiarise visitors with The Age of Goethe. It houses 14 differently themed rooms. Room 1 depicts Frankfurt art of the period – as an artist himself, Goethe often visited the studios of painters in Frankfurt. The next room shows the changing trend from Rococo art to Dutch-style painting at the end of the 18th Century. Room 3 displays the famous painting by the Anglo-Swiss artist, Henry Fuseli, called *The Nightmare*. It depicts a beautiful woman lying in bed in deep sleep with a demonic creature sitting on her bosom and a wide-eyed horse peeping through the curtains. Goethe considered Fuseli a genius and his paintings influenced the *Sturm und Drang* movement, which was characterised by a reaction against rationalism.

Room 5 showcases Goethe's Weimar years and Room 6 explores Rome as the world's academy. Goethe had travelled through Italy and found simplicity and grandeur in its antiquity. He wrote a classic of travel literature called *Italian Journey*.

And so the exhibits went on. But I wanted to hear more about Reza and Rifka finding each other courtesy of Goethe's *West-East Divan*. Reza explained that Goethe looked towards the East for inspiration at a time when many European countries were engaged in fierce battles to establish their empires around the world. Reza believes that the rise and fall of empires creates its own neurosis among the people of the ruling countries. His native country, Iran, was once at the helm of a powerful empire, and their deposed King, Mohammad Reza Pahlavi, was proud that the Persian Empire had spread far and wide. Napoleon, Reza commented, had come to power after the French Revolution and fought many battles to establish a French empire by defeating the Prussians and others but was defeated by the British at Waterloo. When I started working in a hotel in London I'd found it rather unbecoming to advise our French guests to go to Waterloo to catch a Eurostar train to Paris.

"After living and working in Britain for many years," Reza said, "I can only say that many British people haven't really overcome the loss of their empire and it's always present in the back of their minds when they interact with people from former colonies. And of course it was the Nazis' ambition to establish a German Empire that resulted in one of the bloodiest conflicts in human history."

The Goethe House had romantic associations for Rifka and she usually took her friends from abroad to see it when they visited Frankfurt. She teaches at an elementary school in the city and would love to teach Goethe's works to older children. Reza has read both Goethe and Hafez's works in English rather than German and Farsi, being more at home in the language he had learnt at his school in London. "Even though Farsi is my father's first language," Rifka said, "when I was little my father was always humming songs in Farsi while doing chores at home. I never got to learn the language."

I asked Reza to tell me more about his life as a banker in London. He said that he could never forget the day when he lost his job there. In 2008, he had seen many bankers leaving their offices in Canary Wharf carrying their belongings in the cardboard archive boxes known as 'banker boxes' in the stationery trade. But he never imagined that he would suffer the same fate two years later. Reza said that the Faustian pact he had made with the devil was still intact but he was glad that he was now involved in developmental projects rather than speculative financial ventures. "I am always aware, though, that I've sold my soul – not for knowledge but for money," Reza said, pondering his predicament. "But I may seek knowledge in the future if I could put some money aside.'

Reza and Rifka had started a family when they moved

to Frankfurt and their daughter was looked after by Rifka's parents when both of them were at work. Reza said that he had become judicious with his spending ever since the birth of his daughter. "Even though I earn less than I did in the City of London I'm better off in Frankfurt because I spend less money in Germany." Reza said that a lot of Germans do not like the idea of a central bank printing more money because they know too well what could happen if a central bank resorts to printing presses, having never forgotten the absurd enormity of hyperinflation during the time of the Weimar Republic. I recalled that, as a child, I was myself puzzled why the Reserve Bank of India didn't print more money to alleviate poverty in the country.

I told Reza that I had heard that banking in England was started by goldsmiths who gave loans to the merchants and the Crown. He replied that banking families in Frankfurt did the same thing during the 19th Century. My own grandfather was a goldsmith in Kashmir and my grandmother told me that he had been to Jaipur in Rajasthan as a young man to learn how to make fine diamond-studded jewellery. You can say that it was 'an Archimedes guess' for a goldsmith in Kashmir to work out the weight of the gold in a set of jewellery while pricing it for the father of a bride. The goldsmiths were generally distrusted in Srinagar – a saying in Kashmir goes that a goldsmith will con his own mother.

The name of the street where goldsmiths had their shops in Srinagar is borrowed from the Arabic word 'sarraf' which means a money-changer, and in Delhi's Karol Bagh area many goldsmiths have their showrooms in what is known as Bank Street. Every goldsmiths shop during my childhood in Srinagar looked empty except for an iron safe in a corner and a delicate pair of scales on a wooden counter. It was an art to weigh a fraction of an ounce of gold on manual scales. Even a gentle breath of air could tip those scales. A relative told me on a recent trip to Kashmir that his business was ruined by the use of electronic scales because according to him any apprentice could now weigh very small quantities of gold on an electronic machine whereas only an expert goldsmith was able to weigh the precious metal when he worked as an apprentice at his father's shop.

Some of the goldsmiths in Srinagar emptied their safes in the evening and carried the gold coins and jewellery in a metal box in their armpits. My mother likened those businessmen to a barber who came to our home to give a haircut to my grandfather and carried his scissors and blades in a small metal case in his armpit. My grandfather told me that jewellers in Jaipur who sat in small dusty shops when he was there usually opened the safe and took out a rusty box which contained diamonds worth a fortune to show to a client.

I was puzzled as a child when I read the signboards of banks in Srinagar stating that lockers were available. I wasn't at all sure what those lockers were used for until someone told me they were used by account holders for the safekeeping of their gold, and also that some of the goldsmiths in Srinagar stored their own jewellery in them. I always found the fact that a poor country like India was importing tonnes of gold every year bewildering. Most of the gold in India is used as dowry for brides. I had thought the word 'dowry' belonged to one of the languages of the Indian subcontinent until I found this word had its origin in medieval Europe. But the practice is most prevalent in South East Asian countries these days. It is usually the gold that becomes a bone of contention when a marriage doesn't work out. Whenever I hear a tale of marital woes in Kashmir, it brings to mind the lines from Shakespeare's *Romeo and Juliet.*

> 'There is thy gold, worse poison to men's souls,
> Doing more murder to this loathsome world.'

And yes, Goethe had a few things to say on that subject.

Beatrice's Last Smile

Although I'd often visited the state of Baden-Württemberg in southwestern Germany, I'd never before been to Baden-Baden, its well-known spa town. I found its duplicated name curious, like that of Humbert Humbert, the narrator of Nabokov's *Lolita*. A friend in Kashmir liked to call me Iqbal Iqbal and for some time I even used it as my nom de plume in correspondence with friends when I moved to London. I had travelled a few times on the Autobahn that runs through the state from north to south along the Black Forest, which stretches for 99 miles. And I knew Baden-Baden was hidden somewhere in that forest. But it had eluded me for years. In fact, it was Jehangir from Leiman who told me that thousands of people go there, not so much to take the waters as to gamble in the town's casino.

An acquaintance in London had mentioned that Sulieman, a London businessman whom I knew well, had moved to Baden-Baden after filing for bankruptcy in the UK for the second time. It surprised me to hear that he'd become bankrupt again. I thought he was doing well since he owned a small chain of menswear shops in Central London.

They called him Solomon the Wise in the West End. One day, when cycling along Regent Street in the daytime, I noticed that one of his shops was closed. I stopped at a tailoring workshop in the basement of a building in a side road to have a pair of jeans altered and asked Mohammad, who ran the workshop, about Sulieman. He told me that all of Sulieman's shops in London had closed and nobody knew where he had gone. I found Sulieman's visiting card still pinned to a corkboard in Mohammad's workshop. Sulieman used to send him a few trousers and jackets every day to have them altered.

I asked Mohammad if Sulieman owed him any money since he usually paid him every few months. "Not that much," Mohammad said, "not compared to what Sulieman owes his suppliers. Some of them think that he must have spirited money out of the country before filing for bankruptcy." So Sulieman had got into hot water once more. He had lost everything ten years before and then worked as a shop assistant seven days a week in a menswear shop in Regent Street before starting his own business again.

I got to know Sulieman, who is from Kashmir, a couple of weeks after my arrival in London. In those days he ran a shop near Kensington High Street and someone recommended I go to see him as I was looking for work. I rang him and we arranged to meet at his shop at noon the next day. Arriving by Underground, it took me some time to find his shop and I was therefore a bit late for our appointment. I watched Sulieman as he tried to persuade a man to buy a new suit for work and didn't give up until he managed to sell him a pinstripe. It took him half an hour but when he charged £100 on his client's card it put a smile on his face. He was proud of his salesmanship skills.

Before I could properly introduce myself, Sulieman stated that he'd like to give me a valuable tip. "If you want to succeed in finding work, arrive for an appointment before time. Otherwise you've no chance of finding work in a town like London," he said, putting emphasis on the place rather than the timing "The reason I am successful," he claimed, "is because I'm good at timekeeping." He bragged about owning another menswear shop outside London and talked about how much he'd achieved since he arrived in the UK with his British wife eight years earlier. He was an expert salesperson, having worked in a souvenir shop in Mumbai for a number of years. His wife, who was a lot older than him, worked as an accountant in London. She had helped him financially to open a shop in Kensington, which Sulieman referred to as "the Royal Borough of Kensington and Chelsea," presumably to let me know that his shop was located in a classy area. In fact, I was surprised to learn that there was such a thing as a royal borough in London.

It was a big leap for Sulieman to work as a shop assistant in Mumbai and then open his own shop in London. He told me that he usually carried his British passport in his pocket on visits to Mumbai because he was harassed by policemen whenever he accompanied a British or German tourist to the airport. "It was quite a performance applying for a British passport after I moved to London." He referred to the Home

Office, which was based at Lunar House in Croydon, as indeed a lunatic asylum. It felt like a real accomplishment when he finally received his British passport. He felt privileged to be carrying this distinguished-looking, burgundy-coloured document in his pocket. "Since then, I can harass a policeman at Mumbai or Delhi airport instead of anybody in khaki uniform harassing me whenever I go to India."

Sulieman had long hair and sometimes wore a bandana. "The policeman in Mumbai always assumed I was a tout and they'd question me in front of a Memsahib" – an Anglo-Indian portmanteau word combining the 'Ma'am' of English with the 'Sahib' ('sir') of Urdu. The term is still in common use in the Indian subcontinent. When, as a child, I tried to figure out the origin of the word, I thought that an Englishwoman was respectfully called a Memsahib during the Raj because she was usually an Englishman's or Sahib's wife. These days it is sometimes sarcastically used for Indian women of leisure.

I didn't see Sulieman again in London for several years until one day I found him working as a shop assistant in a menswear shop in Regent Street. He was holding up a jacket, waiting for a customer to put it on. He waved at me hesitantly, a bit embarrassed, I think, that I had seen him there. One of his friends had in fact told me that Sulieman had filed for bankruptcy a year earlier and was now working for someone else in Regent Street. I felt sorry that he had lost both of his shops and had been obliged to ask a rival shopkeeper for a job. But Sulieman hadn't lost his passion for selling and I always spotted him on the shop floor attending to newly besuited men whenever I passed the shop where he worked. However, it must have been really tough for him to become a shop assistant after running his own business.

A few years later, I failed to see Sulieman on that shop floor any more and when I asked for him his friend told me that Sulieman had opened his own shop in partnership with his previous manager, Adil, at the other end of Regent Street. He gave me the address and asked me to say hello to Sulieman when I saw him.

I stopped at Sulieman's premises on my next visit to the West End. It was a small shop. Sulieman was dressing a mannequin in the window and was in exuberant spirits once again. In fact, it was his partner who had raised the money for them to open their own shop. Adil had shown faith in Sulieman's highly persuasive sales skills and remortgaged his house to open this small shop in Central London. Adil was from Egypt and was impeccably dressed in a dark suit. He was in charge of the accounts and was also responsible for ordering stock, while Sulieman's responsibility was selling, which was indeed his forte, or, perhaps I should say, his strongest suit. A year and a half later, I passed by Sulieman's shop again and he told me that his business was doing very well; he now employed one or two staff and he was looking to open a second shop in the West End soon.

For the next five years Sulieman and his partner added a shop a year to their portfolio until they owned a total of six shops in and around Central London. It was a fast rise from the ashes for Sulieman to become co-owner of a chain of shops after being a mere shop assistant only a few years before. He spent an hour or so a day in each of his shops demonstrating to the staff how a suit is sold. He told them that no one enters a menswear shop if he wasn't considering buying a new suit and it was therefore their job to ensure that that person buy one. He was certain that no one browses just for the sake of browsing and believed it was the duty of a salesperson to find exactly the right suit for a client. He showed them how to make such a choice, telling them to think of a potential client as a mannequin to be dressed by a fashion designer.

It was a very competitive business selling men's suits in Regent Street. The long-established shops regularly went out of business for failing to afford the high rents imposed by the Crown Estate. Sulieman often told his staff that they could not sell a suit on the basis of the quality of the product alone but had to compete with the big shops in Oxford Street on the strength of their superior customer service. He liked to hang a tape measure around his neck like a lanyard with an attached medal, always carried a box of pearl head-pins, and kneeled on the floor to measure the length of his client's leg from crotch to ankle in order to mark it for alteration. Some of the customers who came into his shop liked the attention he gave them and bought a suit from him. The shopkeeper next door said that Sulieman must be doing something right to have opened half a dozen shops in such a short span of time.

It was past midnight when I happened to see Sulieman outside an Italian restaurant in Covent Garden. He told me that he was waiting for his girlfriend to finish work. I knew that he was in process of getting a divorce from his wife and had started a relationship with another woman a few months ago. This other woman came out of the restaurant while he was talking to me and gave him a kiss on the cheek. He introduced his girlfriend to me as Beatrice. She assumed a haughty manner and something told me that Sulieman's new relationship wasn't going to last long. Beatrice was considerably younger than Sulieman and had long auburn hair. She clutched a small expensive bag in one hand and held Sulieman's hand with the other as they walked to a restaurant in St Martin's Lane. Beatrice was in fact a waitress, not a manageress, as I'd first assumed. I supposed that Sulieman waited for her every night to finish work and then took her to eat in another restaurant.

Sulieman had met Beatrice in a casino in Knightsbridge where she occasionally accompanied a small-time property developer who was a regular at the restaurant where she worked. Sulieman also visited this casino to try his luck with a small bet now and again. He told me that it was one of his well-heeled clients who had introduced him to the casino. Beatrice's property developer companion placed big bets on roulette, mostly lost his money and then left the casino looking morose.

Beatrice has been to Kashmir on holiday a couple of times and was thrilled when she met Sulieman in the casino and learnt he was from Kashmir. He gave her a visiting card and asked her to pop into his shop since they both worked in the West End. He waited for a few days without seeing her and then went to her restaurant on the pretext of having a meal there. She was pleased to see him and Sulieman fell deeply in love with her.

When I met Beatrice for the first time outside that Italian restaurant in Covent Garden, I thought she resembled Manet's model in his *Corner of a Café-Concert*. I had a poster of this painting in my room and when I gazed at it again that evening it revealed an angry expression on the face of the waitress serving drinks.

At this time I was working through the night at weekends near Covent Garden and often saw Sulieman waiting outside the restaurant where Beatrice worked. On one occasion I was sitting in a restaurant in Chinatown when Sulieman and Beatrice walked in and joined me at my table. I asked Beatrice about her visit to Srinagar and she seemed to know quite a few people there. She had stayed in a houseboat on Lake Dal and become friends with the family who owned the boat. She took a Shikara – a small Gondola-like vessel – to cross the lake in the morning and usually found two or three men waiting for her at the wooden platform known as a Ghat. One of them was a doctor and another was a lawyer. The glint in her eye told me that, like Anita Ekberg posing for the paparazzi in *La Dolce Vita*, Beatrice was not averse to that kind of attention. One time I saw a man with his shirt ripped open singing a Bollywood song in the rain on one of the Ghats of Lake Dal. His rendition of this sad old song about unrequited love stopped me in my tracks. As the saying goes in Kashmir: a hard-to-get Memsahib in Lake Dal is a social butterfly who has drunk the water of many Ghats.

Beatrice told me that some of the men she met in Srinagar wrote to her regularly. Such affairs of the heart aren't that uncommon in our town. These men affectionately called Beatrice 'Nuri', meaning in Arabic 'my light' and in Aramaic 'my fire'. Their fascination with Beatrice, I thought, could be compared with Humbert Humbert's obsession with Lolita, whom he describes as 'light of my life, fire of my loins'.

Suleiman also liked to refer to her as his "English rose". In Mumbai, Beatrice was offered work as a model by a businessman who sold saris to Bollywood actresses. She told me that her sari-clad pictures had been published in quite a few magazines in India – Indian men like to see fair-skinned women in such traditional garments. In London, however, she stood no chance of modelling because she was at least four sizes bigger than the average size of models in the UK. The businessman in Mumbai had phoned her recently, she said, and asked her when she was flying to Mumbai because he wanted her to do one more photo shoot for him.

Although Sulieman had been separated from his wife for some time he was still sharing a house with her in East London when he started his relationship with Beatrice. They could therefore only spend nights together by frequenting various hotels in London. Whenever I saw them, Beatrice clung to Sulieman like ivy. He was tall and lean and held Beatrice's head close to his chest while waiting for a cab in the West End in the middle of the night. Sometimes he drove her in his Land Rover.

My excursion to Baden-Baden was literally turbocharged. Jehangir, who lives in Baden-Württemberg, came to pick me up from a hotel in Frankfurt in his sports car. I could have taken a train to Baden-Baden but Jehangir insisted that he drive me there since it wasn't too far – 54 miles – from Leiman, his home-town. Jehangir usually avoids Baden-Baden because of its renowned casino – he doesn't want anyone to think that he goes there to gamble.

I was expecting it to be a winding road because Baden-Baden is located on the side of a hill but it turned out to be as straight as many motorways in Germany. The traffic decreased as we drove through a dark green landscape and the road narrowed before we reached the town. The hotel I'd booked into was located at the corner of the grandly named Beethovenstrasse. Having dropped me off, Jehangir returned to Leiman. He would pick me up again in a couple of days.

Someone in London had given me vague directions where to find Sulieman in Baden-Baden. Unfortunately, the mobile phone number I had didn't exist any more. I walked up and down the main street, Lange Strasse, a few times and then drifted into one of its adjoining streets. Eventually

I struck lucky and came across Sulieman in a boutique. He was understandably startled to see me. I told him that I was visiting the town for a couple of nights and suggested that we meet after he finished work that evening

It is bad enough for anyone to file for bankruptcy once. Hard to imagine, then, what it must have been like to rebuild a business from scratch and then lose it a second time. Sulieman had told me in London that after having been declared bankrupt the first time it was impossible for him to buy a pushbike on credit for years, let alone buy a car or a house. He was without a bank account for several years. "It was a diabolical situation," he said, stressing the word 'diabolical'. I thought of a saying attributed to the Stoic philosopher, Seneca, that 'to err is human, but to persist in error is diabolical'. Sulieman's memory must have been remarkably flawed for him to have trodden the road to bankruptcy for a second time.

I knew it must have been doubly hard for him to have opened so many shops and then lose them altogether. Muhammad had told me that Sulieman ran out of cash at the end and also went through an expensive divorce from his wife. He had used the capital from the first shop to open the second one and invested the capital from the second shop in renting the third. Sulieman's business had become unsustainable after he had opened six shops because banks were unwilling to lend him more money and his chain could not be rescued. He was unable to pay his suppliers and when they stopped sending him merchandise, his shops were half empty and looked it. He tried to borrow money from friends and acquaintances but couldn't raise enough to save his business.

When I asked Muhammad in London about Beatrice, he told me that she had left Sulieman when he needed her most – a couple of weeks before all his shops were sealed and he was again declared bankrupt.

I met Sulieman in a cafe in Baden-Baden after he had finished his work for the day and when we had settled into our conversation I asked him about Beatrice. His expression became profoundly sad at mention of her name. He paused for a few moments before saying, "I saw her in Knightsbridge three weeks after she left me. It was early evening and I was walking along the road – it was just after I'd consulted a bankruptcy lawyer. I was about to pass a casino on the other side of the road when a car came to a halt close by. I saw Beatrice sitting at the front of this old Bentley driven by a man I recognized. He was the property developer she'd known while working as a waitress. When she got out of the car she saw me. She just gave me an odd smile and then walked into the casino holding his arm. Perhaps I would have let it go if she'd been with a man who was the same age as her but the property developer is older than me and as bald as an egg. It was soul-destroying. I decided there and then to leave London – my home city for twenty-five years – for good."

I had known Sulieman as a master of hyperbole when he had Beatrice by his side. For instance, he bragged to me once in Beatrice's presence that the stock in each of his shops was worth "a quarter of a million" rather than saying "two hundred and fifty thousand pounds". But now – no longer working in London – he looked to me like a broken man.

I was curious to know why he had chosen Baden-Baden after deciding to leave London. "Well, the casino was one of the attractions," he admitted. "And the hilly landscape reminded me of Kashmir. The first time I went to Baden-Baden was with a banker who often bought suits at my shop and liked to play poker in casinos in Monaco and Baden-Baden."

Sulieman was accustomed to placing small bets on roulette tables. But he told me that he hadn't set foot inside a casino since moving to Baden-Baden. He showed me a photo dating from his first visit to the town in which he was sporting a big collared shirt unbuttoned at the top. I recalled James Caan playing a professor of English in *The Gambler*, quoting Dostoevsky to his students for inspiration during the day and addicted to gambling in casinos at night. As a matter of fact, Fyodor Dostoevsky lost most of his money playing roulette in a casino in Baden-Baden while working on the manuscript of *The Gambler* at the same time. He had bet the publishing rights of his past and future works and lost the bet.

Incidentally, I had read Dostoevsky's *Crime and Punishment* as a young man in Kashmir but couldn't fully understand the job of a porter in the house where Raskolnikov was living in a garret until I started working as a hall porter in London. When I first visited Camden Town and saw a couple of shops with PAWNBROKER signs, it felt as if I'd arrived in 19th Century St Petersburg.

On my arrival in Baden-Baden, I noticed that the casino was signposted within a bed of flowers at a roundabout. It is called *Kurhaus*, which means 'sanatorium'. I found this name beguiling because it's hard to imagine a casino curing an illness, given that gambling itself can be considered a malady of sorts. There were a lot of Arab tourists out and about, most of them visiting this hillside resort, no doubt, to escape the heat of the Arabian Peninsula in August. Sulieman said that overseas tourists in Baden-Baden had made it easier for him to find a job in the town. He had returned to what he was good at – selling clothes on the shop floor. He chatted to the Arab men and women who walked into the boutique and persuaded them to buy fashion accessories.

While it was certainly painful for Sulieman to talk about losing his shops it was even more painful for him to talk about Beatrice and why she had left him. When I used to see him waiting for her in Convent Garden, I wondered if he had opened so many shops just to impress her. Sulieman didn't care so much about the collapse of his business. It was the loss of his beloved that still troubled him. It had become a metaphor for the loss of London, his home-town. After all, he had spent more years in London than in Kashmir and Mumbai put together. He had taken Beatrice's parents and sister to expensive restaurants whenever they visited. He had even bought a two-bedroom waterfront flat in Limehouse for

Beatrice. "I gave her all the comforts," said Sulieman, "but in the end she was ungrateful."

It was clear that Sulieman still loved Beatrice and wished her well but was tormented by her loss. I asked him if he had returned to London since his relationship with Beatrice ended. "After she left me, I felt as if London itself had betrayed me. I can't bring myself to go back there, even on a short visit. I simply don't have the courage to walk down Regent Street again."

Sulieman had paid for holidays for Beatrice's parents many times, which was one of several reasons why they didn't really mind that their daughter was in a relationship with a very much older man. He also bought expensive jewellery for her mother and gave suits to her father as gifts. Eventually, when he went bankrupt, Sulieman had to pawn his gold watch. He arrived in Baden-Baden wearing one that his friends would have regarded as third-rate.

I asked Sulieman how difficult it was for him to start all over again when he moved to Baden-Baden. "Like other Kashmiris, I learnt my German from tourists visiting Srinagar" he said. "But it was rusty and I had to practice a lot to speak it again. I feel jaded now. I'm not sure if I'll ever run my own business again. Beatrice doesn't need to go back to waitressing to pay for her accommodation because she's still living in the flat that I bought for her outright. That was because she once had to leave her rented flat in the middle of the night and check into a hotel when her landlord who lived in the room next door harassed her." I knew that the Italian owner of the restaurant where Beatrice was working as a waitress was sleeping with one of his staff because he paid the rent of her flat. He was married to an Englishwoman who knew about it but turned a blind eye to his affairs.

When Sulieman talked about Beatrice it was like Dante Alighieri expressing his love for Beatrice Portinari in *The Divine Comedy*. Suleiman quoted a line from a Kashmiri song about the Queen of Sheba being 'the one and only'. "But in the real world, unfortunately, there are all too many moonstruck Suliemans chasing after her. Even now," he said, "when I see a fine-looking blouse in a boutique in Baden-Baden, I think of buying it for Beatrice and sending it to her." He didn't regret having spent a fortune on her. His friends knew that Sulieman had married an Englishwoman in Mumbai to get out of there. But he was consumed by a passionate love for his mistress. "Now I am living in a twilight world and sometimes I think it was all a dream. The other shopkeepers in the West End used to ask me who's that beautiful woman when I walked down the street with her," Sulieman said with a lump in his throat.

The next day Sulieman invited me to have dinner with him in an Indian restaurant on the bank of the River Oos which flows through Baden-Baden. His idea of hospitality hadn't changed even after going through two bankruptcies. I would have liked to pay for both of us. But I was sure that, as a Kashmiri man, he would not have been happy about that. Since I was visiting the town for just a couple of days, he'd feel obligated to be my host. Hospitality is usually elevated to a high moral principle in Kashmir. This was a man, I recalled, who sometimes liked to buy drinks for complete strangers he met in restaurants in London, thus turning them into instant friends.

When I arrived at the restaurant in Lange Strasse, it was already full and there were a few people waiting outside for tables to become free.

Sulieman was unlike his former convivial self when dining out. His manner was subdued and he didn't engage in chit-chat with other people waiting for a table. Eventually we sat at an outside table to eat, talk and watch the water of the Oos flow by. I asked Sulieman about the people who visited the boutique where he works in Baden-Baden. He told me that many wealthy people came to the town to gamble in the casino and there is also a horseracing course that can be reached by a funicular. I was reminded that during my schooldays one of my relatives in Kashmir gained notoriety by betting on horses in Calcutta (now Kolkata). As a matter of fact, the Calcutta racecourse was established in the 19th Century by the British and is therefore considered by some to be a relic of the Raj…

And so, while eating our Indian meal in Baden-Baden, we talked on, meandering from reminiscence to observation to reminiscence as the river flowed before us.

The next morning I went to the boutique where Sulieman works in order to say goodbye. He was in his element, having sold some semi-precious stone jewellery to an Indian lady from Mumbai who was visiting Baden-Baden. When she handed him a credit card to take the payment, he told her that he had worked in a souvenir shop in Mumbai many years ago. He must have been well aware, I thought, that his journey in life was circular, since he had ended up exactly where he started out as an apprentice all those years ago, though now with the added burden of his memories.

As for the burden of mine... I had travelled from Hamburg to Harwich in 1994. Later, having lived in the UK for a number of years, I felt as if I was marooned on a small island. For a long time I regretted my decision to live in the UK rather than settling in Germany. It was my incomprehension of the German language that made me decide to take a ferry to the UK. I thought that I could at least make use of what Nabokov calls 'my second-rate brand of English' if I lived in London. However, as it was for his Russian émigré character, Timofey Pnin, the English idiom proved rather too slippery for my grasp and I lived a sterile life in Hampstead in London for many years. I was unable to find a place among the people in the neighbourhood.

I now felt sympathy for Sulieman who had at least tried twice to build a life in London, albeit on the quicksand of love of a woman who evidently knew the financial value of her beauty.

During those years, I felt that London was devoid of love and I yearned to go back to Kashmir – a paradise that was lost to political turmoil. My only consolation in the last year of the last millennium was to read Proust's *In Search of Lost Time* in a coffee-shop in Hampstead and watch the world go by. I felt somehow elated when I reached the last volume, *Time Regained*, and learnt that 'les vrais paradis sont les paradis qu'on a perdus' – true paradises are the ones that we have lost.

History itself is cyclical, of course, as my travels in Germany had sometimes sadly confirmed. But thanks to its custodians, history bestows upon us memories that are at once burdens and warnings, warnings of where resurgent nationalism can lead us, warnings that might – just might – help us resist falling, into Dante Alighieri's ever-looming inferno.

November 2016 – September 2017

Afterword

When I set out to write this book, I was a little familiar with Germany. My first visit, accompanying my cousin on a business trip, was brief. On the second occasion that I visited, in the early 1990s, I lived there for a few months, and I have visited the country regularly since 2010. However, it proved to be a journey of more significant discovery for me when I travelled to various cities in Germany this time around with the intention of writing a travelogue. I discerned the truth of Proust's saying that 'the real voyage of discovery consists not in seeking new landscapes, but in having new eyes'. I made an effort, at last, to go to see the war memorials in Berlin and Munich and in doing so felt the burden of its history, which I had shied away from when I was living in the country.

Before I started the manuscript, I was back at the beginning of Dante's *Inferno* – 'Midway upon the journey of our life I found myself within a forest dark, for the straight-forward pathway had been lost.' Eleven years had passed since I worked on the manuscript of my last book. The time had been lost and I thought the only way to regain it was to write about the past. And like Calvino's Venetian traveller who conjures up cities for the Chinese ruler, Kublai Khan, I inadvertently travelled back to the city of my own birth – Srinagar.

Acknowledgement:

My sincere gratitude to my editor

Robert Lambolle

for his invaluable support.